EMPHASIZING THE
INTERPERSONAL
IN PSYCHOTHERAPY

EMPHASIZING THE INTERPERSONAL IN PSYCHOTHERAPY

Families and Groups in the
Era of Cost Containment

Claude Villeneuve, M.D.

USA	Publishing Office:	BRUNNER-ROUTLEDGE
		A member of the Taylor & Francis Group
		325 Chestnut Street
		Philadelphia, PA 19106
		Tel: (215) 625-8900
		Fax: (215) 625-2940
	Distribution Center:	BRUNNER-ROUTLEDGE
		A member of the Taylor & Francis Group
		7625 Empire Drive
		Florence, KY 41042
		Tel: 1-800-634-7064
		Fax: 1-800-248-4724
UK		BRUNNER-ROUTLEDGE
		A member of the Taylor & Francis Group
		27 Church Road
		Hove
		E. Sussex, BN3 2FA
		Tel: +44 (0) 1273 207411
		Fax: +44 (0) 1273 205612

EMPHASIZING THE INTERPERSONAL IN PSYCHOTHERAPY: Families and Groups in the Era of Cost Containment

1 2 3 4 5 6 7 8 9 0

Printed by Edwards Brothers, Lillington, NC, 2001.
Cover design by Joe Dieter.

A CIP catalog record for this book is available from the British Library.
∞ The paper in this publication meets the requirements of the ANSI Standard Z39.48-1984 (Permanence of Paper)

Library of Congress Cataloging-in-Publication Data available from the publisher.

ISBN 1-58391-314-9 (paper)

To my family and my fellow therapists.

CONTENTS

PART III
APPLICATIONS OF THE INTERPERSONAL
ORIENTATION

PREFACE

The health care reform under way in Western countries, which is related to the unprecedented inflation in medical services and costs, has already had a profound influence on the delivery of mental health care. We are in a crisis period where pressures from government policy-makers, insurance agencies, and consumer groups are forcing major changes in mental health care delivery in general, and in the practice of psychotherapy in particular. The era of expansion of psychotherapy programs is gone. In the United States managed care programs, which are based on free enterprise and managed competition, reduce their costs by decreasing both access to psychiatric care and the amount of care that is available. This will have a negative impact on the practice of psychotherapy.

To observers from countries where health programs are government-run services and not commodities, the American health system appears "different," to say the least. All Western countries, however, have been practicing one form or another of "managed care" for some time, in terms of shepherding resources and making efforts to manage costs. Even in countries where health delivery is provided through universal health insurance, there are huge efforts to limit the cost of health care. Defined broadly, managed health care means any program that attempts to control the cost of health care. Managed care is only one example of a major transformation that is slowly occurring in the delivery and management of health care in developed countries. To reach this goal, there has been a major shift in orientation toward providing services for a defined population, be it a geographic area or a specific group, and how to meet the needs of that population within very restricted cost limits.

Psychotherapy is at a crossroads. Now may be an appropriate time for psychotherapists to conduct a self-examination, in terms of practicing clinical work in the context of budget cuts.

This is what this book is about. This book will offer the opportunity for clinicians from various orientations to reexamine the relevance of their psychotherapy practice. The shortcomings of some current individual psychotherapeutic approaches will be discussed, and I propose a model based on a larger interpersonal scheme as it applies to families and groups. For example, there is an enormous discrepancy between the positions of some psychoanalysts, with their feelings of the quintessence of their endeavors and the relative limitations of their treatment. Clinical practice is a very complex phenomenon that includes many interacting systems that cannot be reduced to the individual.

The future of psychotherapy is full of uncertainty. Instead of the psychotherapy schools lobbying to determine their importance, it seems that economic factors are more likely to determine the future and the respective importance of each orientation in psychotherapy. It is alarming to realize that some departments of psychiatry have already made psychotherapy training elective. Psychoanalysts have left hospitals and medical schools for private practice, while biological psychiatry reigns in universities and hospitals. The growth of biological psychiatry can be seen as a return to the medical model for the understanding and treatment of psychiatric illness.

In the 1980s, biological research was favored over psychosocial research in the United States. Diagnoses based on psychodynamics and clinical inferences in *DSM-II*, the American Psychiatric Association's *Diagnostic and Statistical Manual of Mental Disorders*, were replaced by the descriptive, more biologically-oriented, and more reliable *DSM-III* classification. The 1990s became the "decade of the brain," further appearing to reduce mental illness to its biological basis. How can one make the best of all these changes and still provide adequate psychotherapeutic services to the patients in this age of public accountability?

The current social and economic changes that affect the practice of psychotherapy are not all negative. Psychotherapy cannot continue to develop while ignoring the social and economic context. Adjustment and innovations are badly needed. Recently, an indigent man told me in tears that his 20-year-old son had been admitted to a psychiatric ward. This man was in deep pain over his son's breakdown, and unable to make sense out of it. No mental health professional had met with him to discuss his son's condition and to help him deal with this trauma.

The practice of psychotherapy must change to prevent it from being reserved for an elite group of patients. The current reform should lead to more diversity in psychotherapy, to developing more effective therapeutic modalities and, hopefully, to a better integration of various approaches. In any case, the development of each individual psychotherapy approach is linked to sociocultural values and is framed by their influence. As we will discuss, these values change over time and psychotherapy practice evolves along with society.

The scarcity of resources may force us to return to more basic practice patterns and to use the resources that exist within natural groups, such as the family and the community, or within groups developed by people with similar interests or problems. Our cultural bias toward individualism has led us to neglect the power of collectivity as a helping resource. Assuming that compassion and mutual aid are no longer important, governments, insurance agencies, and health companies have developed policies and a social security net in an attempt to replace the natural support systems developed by the family, the church, and the neighborhood. Whatever its wisdom, this structure is just a caricature of human relations. It has increased individualism and frustration, and has failed to provide security and down-to-earth support, which are basic elements of human relations.

The emphasis on individual psychotherapy, in particular, has decreased the range of helping behaviors of parents, families, and other human groupings, and has increased peoples' feelings of incompetence and neediness. Under certain conditions, individuals may be able to take more responsibility for themselves and their close relatives, which may help prevent the overuse of individual psychotherapy. Some other incongruities and deficiencies in the practice of psychotherapy call for change. The negative effects of some of our psychotherapy practices are rarely addressed. These topics also will be discussed in this book.

The interpersonal model that will be applied here to families and groups, may complement or occasionally replace traditional psychotherapy for the treatment of certain psychopathological conditions. From the perspective of health care providers, these interpersonal therapies may be more cost effective than individual treatment. In conjoint family therapy, for example, the intervention is not focused only on the index patient but also on the other family members' well being. Group and family therapies are often brief, structured, and problem focused, characteristics which particularly well suit the current and predicted trend in the practice of psychotherapy. These therapeutic modalities easily can be added to other clinical approaches as specific interventions tailored to specific problems.

Problems that are often not adequately tackled by individual psychotherapy, such as those of young adolescents, the elderly, people with personality disorders, and those with chronic mental illness will be reviewed using the interpersonal perspective, and translating relevant knowledge through the interpersonal lens. It is striking to realize how little the families of patients with personality disorders or of patients with chronic mental illnesses are made part of the treating team, and the ordeal that they go through is poorly dealt with. The popularity of self-help groups, which also testifies to the limitations of our current psychotherapeutic practice, also will be discussed.

The interpersonal model will also be used to fill in the gaps between various psychotherapeutic approaches and to foster their integration. Since the theoretical input of Kernberg and Kohut and the development of cognitive therapy, there has been no new development in the field of individual psychotherapy theory, to the point of near stagnation. The future of psychotherapy seems to rest more on integrating and combining approaches.

Current trends in the practice of psychotherapy lean towards the integration of what is known and already practiced. The more severe and disruptive the illness, the greater the need to include multiple components and to integrate the family into the treatment. In any case, the current threat to psychotherapy practice may lead to the discovery of common ground and alliances among the psychotherapy approaches. Most psychotherapies, as we will see, are not mutually exclusive, and group and family approaches share common curative factors with the individual interventions. The practice of psychotherapy must change as health care reform, managed care programs, and cost containment give more importance to short-term interventions. These changes should foster the use of group and family therapy.

My training, teaching, and clinical practice have given me the opportunity to experiment with very different perspectives in psychotherapy including individual, group, and conjoint family therapy. I trained at the Canadian Psychoanalytic Institute, where the British, the French, and the American schools of psychoanalysis are taught. I worked in two universities in Montreal, each different in their orientation toward psychotherapy.

This book is the culmination of what I have learned from working with various therapeutic orientations. Like most clinicians, the impact of clinical practice on my theoretical orientation has been substantial. I began my career with the idea of doing analysis and intensive psychodynamic psychotherapy with children and adults. It became evident that the psychoanalytic treatment of children, in particular, implied working with a very special group of people. The children referred to me were from families in which one or both parents were already in analysis themselves and firmly believed that their child also could benefit from the same treatment. I could not work within such a therapeutic subculture, ignoring the needs of the majority of psychiatric patients, and my own transition into interpersonal therapy started there. I did not stop doing analysis altogether.

I also felt uneasy seeing the same people accompanying patient week after week (and sometimes year after year), and having nothing to do but sit in the waiting room until the end of the psychotherapy session. It reminded me of medical clinics where relatives are kept away from the treatment process. These people showed great admiration and reverence to the psychotherapist, who was perceived as having the power to cure the patient. I always thought the time they spent at the clinic could be more constructively used by finding a way of involving them in the treatment.

To highlight the contradictions and the incongruities of certain psychotherapy practices, some observations made in this book may seem provocative. It is difficult to deal with these issues without hurting individual susceptibilities, as most psychotherapists fiercely defend one particular approach. This makes psychotherapy paradoxical, as there is no evidence that any particular approach is superior to the others. However, this statement needs to be nuanced, as many factors are involved. For example, the therapeutic goals set for psychotherapy vary between approaches and even within the same approach. This book is not intended, however, to underestimate the primacy of individual psychotherapy. Nor is it intended to give ammunition to those who oppose psychotherapy and want to replace it with a more biological and mechanistic view of emotional problems.

This volume is intended for clinicians from various disciplines who may have to modify the way they practice psychotherapy because of the current health care reform and the shift in care toward severe psychiatric problems and shorter interventions. It should also be of value to students in the mental health field who, sooner or later, will be influenced by these reforms. This book should be beneficial, as well, to those who already use the interpersonal perspective but whose work is under-valued and sometimes not even seen as psychotherapeutic.

THE FIELD OF PSYCHOTHERAPY

1

CHAPTER

Overview

Psychotherapy is not a modern invention, although its scientific foundations have only recently been laid out. As a social entity, however, psychotherapy may be too narrow in its present form to endure deep social change. This chapter briefly describes the evolution of psychotherapy and discusses why individual psychotherapy in the Western world has become a social phenomenon whose importance deserves a closer look. The current transformation of psychotherapy under socioeconomic pressures are then presented. Finally, the efficacy of various forms of psychotherapy, including group and conjoint family therapy (which cannot be ignored by governments and tax payers) and their common curative factors are briefly reviewed.

☐ Defining Psychotherapy

Psychotherapy can be defined as a professional form of intervention focusing on alleviating psychological distress and psychological and behavioral dysfunction, through verbal methods and interpersonal actions, conducted with individuals or small groups (Ford & Urban, 1998). Psychotherapy is a generic term covering a wide spectrum of therapeutic modalities that can be grouped into individual versus collective (family, group) psychotherapies. Psychotherapy can also be defined as focusing mostly on the intrapsychic (e.g., psychodynamic psychotherapy) or mostly on the interpersonal (e.g., group and conjoint family psychotherapy).

According to Frank (1982), psychotherapy incorporates the following features: 1) a trained healer, whose efficacy is recognized by the sufferer and his social group; 2) a sufferer who seeks relief from the healer; 3) a series of contacts between the healer and the sufferer, through which the healer, often with the aid of a group, attempts to change the affective state or behavior of the sufferer. The change is brought about mainly by words or actions in which the sufferer, the healer, and the group (if any) participate.

It is interesting to note that these features are also present in primitive healing and in religious conversions. As Frank (1982) noted, healing rites usually require the participation of the family or the social group, and the group presence has been a feature of most religious-magic healing rituals. The ideology of the Western world, which fosters autonomy and self-sufficiency, has modeled the use of psychotherapy, with the shift from a group to an individual orientation to achieve freedom from within and without.

☐ Evolution of Psychotherapy

The role of the psychotherapist is not new. People have always looked to someone else for help and, throughout time, there have been people devoted to improving the well being and alleviating the mental distress of their fellow citizens through "psychological" means, from the shaman or medicine man, to the religious leader, to today's psychotherapist. As commented by Ehrenwald (1976), every society includes individuals who are perceived as being able to help with emotional problems, using magical, religious, or scientific methods.

Freud's work was the great turning point in the history of psychotherapy, ending one era and beginning a new one. In his work, Freud gave a scientific basis to what healers of all kinds had practiced on individuals with physical or psychic pain. Freud broke away from the theories of positivism and the Age of Reason of Descartes. He approached madness through language, an experience reduced to silence by positivists, and opened the possibility of a dialogue with the *déraison* and further rapprochement with the mentally ill (Foucault, 1973). Freud posited the supremacy of the unconscious as a driving force.

Psychoanalysis was an attempt to eliminate emotional problems through focusing on the intrapsychic. Freud presented new theories which became new dogmas. Freud's theory created great enthusiasm, bringing the idea that emotional disorders could be cured by psychological means. After World War II, psychoanalysis exerted a great influence upon psychiatry and other clinical disciplines.

Eventually, this brought disillusionment, especially in the United States. Freud's focus on the unconscious as the motivating force of human functioning led to a backlash with other positions that focused on conditioning theory and on interpersonal behavior as the main motivating forces. Part of the backlash to psychoanalysis was the development of the existential–humanist movement which led to a multitude of new psychotherapies, often conducted in groups, based on the idea that talking was not enough.

During World War II, mental health workers from various disciplines were trained to do short psychotherapeutic interventions with soldiers who had to return to the front. This trend also favored the pioneer work of group therapists, such as Slavson (1943), in search of a practical way to meet the increasing demand for therapy. After the war, there were also successful attempts to shorten psychoanalytic treatment, which gave rise in the 60s and 70s to brief psychodynamic psychotherapy. During the same period, conjoint family therapy based on von Bertalanffy's (1968) systems theory brought a new perspective on human problems by emphasizing the context in which psychopathology develops, breaking away from the view of treating the individual in isolation. Bateson and Erickson contributed to the development of strategic short-term therapies (Haley, 1976).

The last few decades have seen a move toward the subjectivation of the field of psychotherapy, away from the emphasis on science. The objectivity of the analyst and the "blank screen" have given way to intersubjectivity and the importance of countertransference. Classical behavior therapy has moved toward a cognitive approach, even though the humanistic–experiential approaches, which emphasize subjectivity, have decreased in importance (Bergin & Garfield, 1994).

The development of psychotherapy is also linked to the changes in mental health service delivery in the last century in Western countries. The 20th century has witnessed many revolutions in the delivery of psychiatric services: In the first half of the century, psychiatry was practiced in hospitals, while, in the last four decades, the practice has moved toward home care and community-based settings with the increased involvement of families and groups. The current health care reform brings a new orientation to mental health care delivery, with a re-examination of the role of psychotherapy. As one will see in this book, the status of psychotherapy is still changing. Psychotherapy has lost its primacy and glamor and is now seen as one of several treatment modalities—in some treatment centers, its usefulness is even questioned.

Can we afford to lose the human element of the relationship between the healer and the sufferer, which has been at the core of the therapeutic relationship since the birth of humanity? As expressed by Holmes (1994), "psychotherapy epitomizes the values of the doctor–patient relationship, of healing as opposed to treating, that patients and doctors alike find so elusive in modern medical culture" (p. 1071). The human element of psychotherapy may be more important than ever.

☐ Predominance of Individual Psychotherapy

The importance of psychotherapy in modern times cannot be overemphasized. It is estimated that one third of the U.S. population has used psychotherapy at some point in their lives, and there may be as many as 250,000 psychotherapists, including counsellors, available (Vandenhos, Cummings, & Deleon, 1992). There are probably more psychotherapists today than ever in Western society.

As Cushman (1995) commented, individual psychotherapy is central to Western culture and it appeals to both the patient and the therapist. We do not even contextualize it; we treat it as though it is a transhistorical science that treats universal illnesses. Because we are blinded by the ideal of individualism, which is part of our cultural heritage, it is hard to see the impact of individual psychotherapy on our formulations. Psychotherapy is even used by some people as the main problem-solving tool.

Social conditions and one's way of life are assumed to play an important role in the place given to individual psychotherapy. Psychotherapy has developed at a time when the traditional ways of living and social norms have diminished in importance. Cushman (1992) argues that the psychotherapist is asked to deal with the consequences of fragmentation and alienation that plague modern people and the disintegration of the family. In a febrile attempt to get rid of these problems, individuals go to the specialist of the mind as the source of their cure.

The end of feudal society allowed people to move around freely. This resulted in the move toward cities, and thus, people being more separated from tradition and family. As described by Cushman (1995), this led to discontinuity, to isolation of the self, and losing one's guidepost. The individuals lost their community and its shared meanings, and this imperative to make their own choices evolved into a need for psychotherapy. People now have to find the answers that used to come from external sources. As Taylor (1992) argues in *Malaise of Modernity*, we even have to discover and formulate our own identity, whereas before the era of choices, our lifestyles and niches were preordained, as a part of a whole which was determined by external forces. The locus of control and transcendence moved from the outside to within (Cushman, 1992).

The need for individual psychotherapy can then be understood as a way to help one face the very strong move toward the many forms of subjectivation in modern culture. According to Taylor (1989), in the past 200 years, the self has become more individualistic and more subjective, a decontextualized individual self. The subject becomes the center of everything. This freedom and autonomy force one to center on oneself. The unknown, which was thought to be located on the outside, was slowly perceived to be within the self, the repressed primitive drives of Freud's theories.

In consequence, our cultural ethos is that of self-contained individualism (Sampson, 1993). Western society created the image of the individual as being self-soothing and self-sufficient. This phenomenon isolates individual from individual, although interdependence is at the basis of human development. The self-contained individual has firm self–nonself boundaries and high personal control (Sampson, 1993). These characteristics are, however, quite subjective and vary on a continuum crossculturally (Baumeister, 1987). In other cultures, these traits are often conceptualized within an interdependent collectivity, such as the family.

The individualistic values of modern societies influence psychotherapists who emphasize personal needs and self-expression. These values are given precedence over the family and the community. In the mental health field, the view of a self-contained individual is predominant (Cushman, 1995). Moreover, the interests of the individual practitioner and of the professions have certainly played a role in the choice of the modality and the patients seen in psychotherapy. Most psychotherapists prefer to work with individuals instead of families or groups of patients. This practice is less strenuous and more predictable.

In individual psychotherapy, the focus is on self. The individualistic, self-contained ideal is often re-inforced, decreasing the importance of interdependent values. Open-ended psychodynamic psychotherapy epitomizes the ideology of the self-contained individual. The patient is separated from his environment and cared for within the patient–therapist relationship.

In Western society, particularly in the United States, the business of psychotherapy is a mental health industry with a relatively homogeneous practice. The cultural and historical ways of dealing with emotional problems, such as using the family and other natural groups, are partly ignored. The practice of individual psychotherapy has become a subculture with its own beliefs and economic interests, determining the ways to cope with psychological distress.

A good example of the above practice is the way in which mental health practitioners deal with bereavement and grief. Grief is perceived as a private experience with a specific endpoint and prescribed detachment, even though the process of grief on a prescribed timeline seems to be contradicted by empirical research (Wortman & Silver, 1989). The focus in bereavement is on the individual experience instead of the family and the sociocultural context that is linked to the family.

A middle-aged widow referred her only child, a 16-year-old daughter, for individual psychotherapy because she thought the girl was experiencing a depression related to her father's death. The father, who had been the family's dominant figure, died in a car accident one year previously.

The conjoint interview revealed a gloomy and depressing family atmosphere. Both women were sad, especially the mother, and it was obvious that they were still grieving. The memory of the father was still vivid in both women's minds, but they had been unable to share their pain. The mother had seen a therapist shortly after her husband's death but her daughter's condition was not ever discussed. The individual was given precedence over the family, and no effort was made to link the mother to her natural support system. The mother had been unable to regain her previous level of functioning. She was surprised, however, to hear her daughter report how her mother changed after the father's death—being unable to keep a job, withdrawing and refusing social invitations. Both had a negative influence on each other's ability to mourn. The daughter was forced to play a parenting role, which kept her close to her depressed parent. She greatly resented this role and was openly criticized by her father's family for doing it. The mother felt the need to protect and be close to her daughter, which prevented both women from reinvesting in other relationships and life pursuits.

Instead of offering individual help to the daughter to complete her grieving, which would have been the intervention expected within the therapeutic culture, the clinician explored the family environment. Then, the clinican used this environment both as a target of intervention and as a resource to help with the problem, which probably showed a faster result and used less outside resources. The mother and daughter were seen together on a weekly basis for a few months and were invited to share their common memories as well as some of their private experiences with the deceased father. The culture of the father's family was still permeating the family process. In this family, women were not allowed to take initiative. With the opening of the family system, the daughter was slowly relieved of the burden of helping her mother. The feelings of guilt and helplessness that had plagued the daughter quickly lifted.

Evolutionary biology is another perspective that could highlight the need for psychotherapy. According to theories based on evolutionary biology, the mismatch between genes and environment could be seen as a major source of psychological distress. Our genes are assumed to have been formed in an era when for hundreds of thousands of years, men were nomads, hunter-gatherers living in small bands, closely bound to each other for survival. This harsh environment has changed, but genes have not. Glantz and Pearce in their book, *Exiles from Eden, Psychotherapy from an Evolutionary Perspective* (1989), give an example of this mismatch: our current child-rearing practices, which, they theorize, could lead to psychological problems. In the hunting and gathering environment, children had frequent contacts with many supportive adults, relatively long nursing, and a go-at-your-own-pace learning. The genetically coded needs related to these practices can hardly be met now. Therefore, children are in need of rearing practices that are usually unavailable today.

Individual psychotherapy seems to meet other current needs. It relates in particular to the current dissatisfaction of patients with medical treatments that neglect the doctor–patient relationship. This dissatisfaction has its roots in the fact that patients suffer from the conflict between medicine's relational aspects and the new medical technology.

Our focus on the experience of the individual and on limited psychotherapeutic sources is of concern when we consider the variety of problems, the ways of living, and the cultures of people presenting psychological distress, such as immigrants (see chapter 2). Psychotherapy has traditionally tried to promote change in one individual without much effort to involve his or her larger system to facilitate the change.

☐ Current Changes

We are witnessing important changes in psychotherapy practice related to a variety of socioeconomic and scientific factors. Economic forces are certainly not negligible in the structure of psychotherapy. There is already an emphasis on accountability that has placed cost-effectiveness at the core of mental health care programs. In the United States, one of the most important economic causes is the advent of regulatory devices such as diagnostic-related groups (DRGs). DRGs control hospitalization costs by paying according to estimates based on diagnosis instead of on other factors such as the complexity and severity of the cases. Another important market-based strategy is the corporate for-profit regulation of medical care, which is taking over health care management. Companies provide services to groups of citizens through health maintenance organizations (HMOs) and replace the traditional fee-for-service model. This is an era of economic-driven mental health care programs with a lot of variation in their modalities of application.

Today's health care planners tend to remain within the individualistic tradition, neglecting the family perspective in primary medical care settings with issues such as home-based care and the reorganization of services. The reorganization of mental health care delivery based on collaboration and the use of the family as a target for intervention has been pushed aside, as well as the preventative perspective, which is also emphasized when the family unit is involved.

In most Western countries, the health care challenges mental health workers, especially psychiatrists, to redefine their professional responsibilities and to consider the treatment of the individual in the context of the needs of the population at large. As discussed by Olfson and Pincus (1994), this has a tremendous impact on psychotherapy practice, especially on long-term psychotherapy. As psychotherapy was practiced until a few decades ago in an unregulated way, there are now requirements, such as establishing criteria for therapy and an endpoint for treatment.

According to the Committee on Therapy for the Group for the Advancement of Psychiatry (GAP, 1992), long-term exploratory psychotherapy will be scrutinized and probably excluded from the roster of reimbursable treatments, and emphasis will be put on low-cost services such as time-limited and symptom-focused interventions. Corporate health managers find it difficult to cope with the concept of open-ended psychotherapy, since they follow the medical model in which many physical illnesses and medical procedures are predictable in terms of time and accountability.

Most predictions of the future of psychotherapy, including those made by a panel of 75 experts in the field of psychotherapy (Norcross, Alford, & DeMichele, 1992), foresee that the health care dollar will likely be the main force behind the type of psychotherapy used. This implies that short-term intervention, done individually, conjointly, or in groups will be the therapy modality of choice, as time is becoming the major consideration. This modality has already become the modal form of treatment (Garfield & Bergin, 1994).

The differences in point of view and actual practice between the short-term and long-term orientations to psychotherapy has been well spelled out by Budman and Gurman (1988). In short-term interventions, a focus is actively maintained, circumscribed goals are set, and resistance and negative transference are quickly handled. Therapists do not try to change the patient's character structure. They often emphasize strength and resources, and hope for changes to happen outside of the session. Therapists with a long-term orientation usually believe that changes comes with more sessions, and these changes are closely monitored and guided during sessions (Budman & Gurman, 1988). Most clinical vignettes presented in this book illustrate the use of brief interventions, even though in some cases the problem presented would logically require longer interventions (for example, see the case of Jason in chapter 6).

In any case, epidemiological studies (e.g., Lambert & Hill, 1994) reveal that the substantial majority of patients have a short course of psychotherapy, even though much of the database antedates managed-care programs. As reported by MacKenzie (1990), the psychotherapy attendance curve shows that approximately two-thirds of the patients in outpatient programs are seen for six sessions or less, and less than 10% are in treatment for more than 25 sessions

In their book espousing a "family practice" approach to psychotherapy, Budman and Gurman (1988) argue that a good proportion of patients, including those who received intensive psychoanalytic psychotherapy, have recurrent episodes of therapy. Based on this fact, they consider that unplanned brief psychotherapy is often used. Reviewing outcome research in time-limited psychotherapy, MacKenzie (1990) shows that the shortness of the intervention is not an handicap in terms of efficacy (see also Howard, Kopta, Kraus, & Orlinsky, 1986). In fact, the outcome literature and the poor attendance curve justify a greater use of time-limited interventions, including group and conjoint family therapy. These findings will be studied in this book in regard to some patient groups with a tendency toward poor attendance to individual psychotherapy.

As a consequence of the changes described in this chapter, the importance of the family and of fellow patients in the treatment of the emotionally ill has considerably decreased. The natural law of mutual aid has been replaced by the law of justice and adversarial systems, by individualism, and, now, by the dictates of economic planning and scientific discoveries

☐ Efficacy of Different Psychotherapies

Much of the research in psychotherapy focuses on its efficacy. In the first place, the efficacy of psychotherapy has to be evidenced so as to fight the popular belief that it is ineffective. The viability of psychotherapeutic approaches also has to be demonstrated to taxpayers, governments, and insurance companies. Since Eisenck (1952) claimed that patients receiving psychotherapy fared no better than those who were waiting for treatment, numerous studies have proved the efficacy and the cost-effectiveness of psychotherapy (see Bergin & Garfield, 1994). The use of meta-analysis (grouping studies together) has been a popular research strategy for evaluating the efficacy of psychotherapy, including group and conjoint family therapy. The results of some these meta-analytic studies will be presented in various parts of this book, to show the therapeutic strength of conjoint family and group therapy.

The field of psychotherapy research has reached a good degree of sophistication. A research methodology has been developed to define requirements for proper research design concerning psychotherapy outcome. These criteria are now well elucidated (Klerman & Weissman, 1993):

1. Randomized clinical trial design
2. Structured interviews for assessing inclusion criteria
3. Large sample size to ensure statistical power
4. Use of manuals to standardize the therapy practiced and ensure proper therapists' training
5. Use of multiple observers besides the therapist or the patient
6. Use of multiple dimensions of symptoms and functioning (measuring psychopathology, social functioning, and quality of life)

As discussed below, the use of various dimensions of the problem presented is very important in regard to the debate between the tenets of short-term versus long-term psychotherapy. Symptom reduction and social functioning are not equivalent. Social functioning, which includes adaptive behavior, participation in social activities, and making friends is also a major, albeit different, indicator of improvement (Kazdin, 1994a).

In their review of outcome research on the effectiveness of psychotherapy, Lambert and Bergin (1994) concluded that the differences in outcome between various forms of psychotherapy are not as important as one might have expected. When strict criteria are used (such as a control group, some form of active treatment for the control group, and a longer follow-up period) meta-analytic research has demonstrated that only a minimal portion (10–12%) of outcome variance is accounted for in the therapeutic approach used and its method and techniques.

In a meta-analytic study, Luborsky and associates (1993) compared psychoanalytic psychotherapy to behavioral, cognitive–behavioral, cognitive, experiential, and group therapy; they found these approaches equally effective. Thirteen comparative studies were lumped together and only reliable well-known outcome measures were used. In addition, the dosage–response work done by Howard and colleagues (1986) also gives weight to brief interventions. This outcome research showed that half of the people in psychotherapy show significant improvement by the eighth session and that most patients get optimal improvement within 26 sessions. These studies give more credit to group and conjoint therapies, which are usually of short-term duration.

For interpersonal problems, meta-analytic studies showed that conjoint and group therapies are more effective than alternatives such as individual psychotherapy (see chapters 4 and 5). Even in randomized studies comparing conjoint therapy to individual psychotherapy, for some problems not traditionally dealt with by conjoint therapy such as anxiety and medical problems, no differences were found (Shadish, Ragsdale, Glaser, & Montgomery, 1995; see chapter 4).

The idea that various psychotherapeutic approaches yield the same therapeutic results has raised a lot of debate. These controversies have centered mostly on the use of short-term versus long-term psychotherapy. In defense of long-term psychodynamic psychotherapy, many argue (for example, Doidge, 1997; Gabbard, 1994) that it is hard to conduct comparative studies of short-term versus long-term psychotherapies. Short-term psychotherapy usually focuses on circumscribed symptomatic problems and not on personality pathology or chronic problems.

These authors also assert that most measures used tap symptoms and neglect larger areas such as the patients' quality of life and emotional growth, which may be considered essential in regard to the complexity involved in the overall effectiveness of therapy. Acccordingly, there is evidence that short-term psychotherapy is more effective in relieving symptoms than in increasing adaptive functioning and bringing about character change (Gabbard, 1994). The combination of character disorders and symptoms (Axis I and Axis II comorbidity), for example, often does not respond to short-term psychotherapy and requires a long-term approach (Doidge, 1997).

In addition, Doidge (1997) explained that evidence-based research has led investigators to use "manualized" approaches at the expense of exploratory interventions and creativity, and that the criteria set for outcome research forced therapists to focus on short-term approaches at the expense of longer-term psychodynamic psychotherapy. "Manualized" treatment is somewhat inconsistent with the philosophy of long-term psychodynamic psychotherapy.

As reported by Doidge (1997), other factors make it difficult to evaluate the efficacy of long-term psychoanalytic psychotherapy and psychoanalysis. While efficacy studies are based on a fixed number of sessions, psychoanalytic therapy is open-ended and lasts until the patient has improved. These modalities treat comorbid conditions as well, necessitating a more complex design for evaluation. For ethical reasons, it is difficult to use waiting lists as control groups for long-term psychotherapy compared with short-term psychotherapy (Doidge, 1997).

Parallel to evidence-based psychotherapy research, undertaken mostly by researchers doing short-term psychotherapy with well-delineated protocols, there is a second type of research tradition, based on long-term psychotherapy and mostly done by clinicians espousing the psychoanalytic model. As described by Shapiro and Emde (1995), these researchers conceive their clinical material as comprehensive, longitudinal, and multifactorial, and consider that outcome measures do not usually tap themes that should theoretically favor psychodynamic psychotherapy. An increasing body of research related to basic psychoanalytic concepts has emerged (for a review, see Henry, Strupp, Schacht, & Gaston, 1994).

In any case, both traditions in psychotherapy research have to be considered in an overall understanding of the efficacy of psychotherapy. There is, however, a consensus that the efficacy and cost-effectiveness of long-term individual psychotherapy has not been fully established. Most of the relevant studies have serious methodological problems: lack of controls, unrepresentative samples, therapist's judgments sometimes used as the main measure of outcome.

Long-term therapy does not necessarily imply open-ended individual psychodynamic psychotherapy. Conjoint and group therapy also may be done on a long-term basis and can be exploratory and growth-promoting to produce basic changes in the intrapsychic and the relational environment of the patient.

☐ Common Curative Factors

Many controversies and debates also exist about the specific versus nonspecific factors involved in the efficacy of psychotherapy. What are the critical ingredients in successful psychotherapy? This elusive question has been addressed in psychotherapy research. The fact that major forms of psychotherapy have equal efficacy has led researchers to look for nonspecific factors transcending the various psychotherapeutic orientations that are common to most approaches.

The commonalities between the various orientations cannot be ignored any longer as the effective components appear to be much less specific than some therapists want to believe. Beutler and colleagues (1994) comment that there is a contradiction in the fact that most of what is written about psychotherapy concerns its orientation, which only accounts for a small percentage of changes achieved. Garfield and Bergin (1994) enumerate common curative factors found in various forms of psychotherapy: the therapeutic relationship, the creation of hope, the possibility of emotional release, the interpretations and explanations of one's problems, cognitive changes, advice, support, and testing new behaviors.

It is accepted by most psychotherapeutic orientations that the therapeutic relationship is of prime importance in psychotherapy (Lambert & Bergin, 1994). This view is based on the assumption that if relationships are essential to human being, they are also essential to correct relationship disturbances. The therapeutic relationship includes not only the therapist–patient relationship, but also includes the relationship between group or family members in interpersonal therapies. In his review of research in this field, Dies (1994) concludes that intermember bonding often is more important than the relationship between the group therapist and the members of the group.

The therapeutic relationship depends not only upon the patient's unconscious defenses and transference distortions but also upon the "real" interpersonal relationship and the attributes of the patient and the therapist that are, according to psychotherapy research, the most important determinants of efficacy (for a review, see Beutler et al., 1994). Various therapist characteristics have been proved to be related to positive therapeutic outcomes in a large number of empirical studies (Beutler et al., 1994). Good therapists develop an empathic and accepting relationship with their patients, and they exhibit warmth; they give their patients the feeling of being cared for and valued. Their effectiveness also appears to be related to being responsive and active, which contributes to a good interpersonal relationship (Beutler et al., 1994).

This may give an edge to conjoint and group therapy, conferring more credit to concrete interpersonal interventions which emphasize the "real" relationship of the therapist and of the other participants and their responsiveness. The importance of "real" interpersonal relationships is manifested in many of Yalom's (1995) factors to explain the efficacy of group therapy. It is interesting to note that the notion of interpersonal relationships as a curative factor is also shown in healing marriages. Lewis (1998) demonstrated that the marital relationship can be a healing process to undo the consequences of very negative childhood experiences. Reviewing the literature on interpersonal relationships in regard to healing marriages and well-functioning families, Lewis (1998) sees a common thread between these and effective psychotherapy. They are all based on intimate interpersonal relationships emphasizing respect for subjective reality, empathy, and warmth.

Comparing insight to action (i.e., trying out new behavior), Wachtel (1987) argues that both are linked to the efficacy of psychotherapy and that both should be enhanced. In a circular causality model, insight and action form a recursive loop. To Wachtel, when insight brings a new meaning to a certain behavior, the behavior is more likely to change. Conversely, the emergence of new behaviors in a relationship may change the meaning of the relationship. This loop is important and can be easily seen in interpersonal psychotherapy.

However, paraphrasing Bergin and Garfield (1994), the common factors approach and the "no differences" of meta-analytic studies cannot erase the fact that there is specific and superior efficacy of some approaches with specific problems, for example, behavioral and cognitive approaches with phobias and compulsions. Psychotherapy practice and research has thus reached some level of precision that enables therapists to specify which form of psychotherapy to use, for which problem, and for which individual. This specificity is better evidenced for individual psychotherapy, while it has not been fully explored for group and conjoint family approaches.

Shortcomings of
Individual Psychotherapy

The psychodynamic body of knowledge that has derived from Freud's work and method of investigation has proved to be powerful in the understanding and treating of psychological suffering. However, the very important theoretical contribution of psychoanalysis has not resulted in universal access to adequate psychotherapy. Among the general public, the level of confidence in psychoanalysis and its derivative, open-ended psychotherapy, is on the decline (Garfield & Bergin, 1994). Young psychoanalysts struggle to find patients. With the economic and social upheavals, open-ended psychotherapy is poorly-funded. Already, many private health insurance providers do not pay for it. Will open-ended psychotherapy be available only for those who can afford it? The factors leading to this will now be discussed. Some theoretical and practical difficulties in the use of most types of individual psychotherapy, such as their limited applicability, will also be reviewed.

☐ Fascination with Psychoanalysis

Psychoanalysis and psychodynamic psychotherapy fascinated generations of clinicians at a time when there were few therapeutic alternatives. This fascination became detrimental when the tremendous success of psychoanalysis as a method of exploration made some clinicians believe that it must be the quintessential way to conduct psychotherapy, and possibly the only meaningful response to a variety of clinical problems. Exploration with other psychotherapeutic modalities was deemed unnecessary, which could explain in part the relative paucity of psychotherapeutic alternatives until recently.

Since the relief of symptoms has to be postponed for a greater motive (in both psychoanalysis and dynamic psychotherapy), any psychotherapy that insisted on symptom relief was seen as antithetical to analysis, and as catharsis and suggestion based on subjective improvement. Psychoanalysis is still sometimes presented as the only model of psychotherapy that seeks meaning and is humanistic. Amazed by the material emerging in their private offices, some analysts upheld the belief that psychoanalysis is an entity that cannot be confronted by knowledge coming from other disciplines, even though the findings of developmental psychology have helped to change psychoanalytic theory.

☐ Freud and Linear Causality

Linear causality and elements of the closed-system view of human functioning are used in Freud's theories. As these theories have been updated, it may not be useful here to discuss this topic in depth. We will, however, mention a few key elements, as traditional Freudians still assume that some elements of psychological life are immune from further influence and are cut off because of early repression. This assumption has often led to the neglect of the interpersonal and the present. To Wachtel and McKinney (1992), unconscious wishes and fantasies are treated as "givens" from the past. They make their way to the present intact and serve to explain current behavior, as if the present is not in interinfluence with the unconscious past, when accounting for the behavior of the individual. These traditional analysts are prisoners of linear thinking in a nonlinear world. Within a biopsychosocial model, circularity is almost inevitable. Each human component is part of an hierarchically-organized whole—the individual—which functions through the circularity of his or her interactive parts.

The traditional view of the psychoanalytic process is based on a closed-system linear causality model. The nature of the analytic situation fosters the unfolding of the unconscious, and showing that the patient's productions have little to do with the present but rather come from the past, confirm the analyst's assumption. In the psychoanalytic setting, the environment is reduced to a minimum and kept constant. The couch, the relative non-responsiveness of the analyst, and the patient's free associations all contribute to the expression of the unconscious past and its apparent supremacy. As the analysand leaves the analytic room, however, the interpersonal environment resumes its place, and the equilibrium between the intrapsychic and the interpersonal environment is replaced.

☐ Limitations of Individual Psychotherapy

The sole emphasis on individual treatment is particularly problematic when the patient depends upon others because of age (a child, a younger adolescent, an older patient) or mental condition. Psychodynamic psychotherapy, for example, is only applicable to a small portion of the psychiatric population, namely individuals who are interested in self-exploration. Refraining from structure and feedback allows the unfolding of the patient's unconscious, and may bring too much anxiety to some patients who cannot tolerate ambiguity.

Both brief and open-ended traditional psychodynamic psychotherapy cannot be used with seriously ill people because they do not have the capacity to work the transference. Most psychiatric patients need explicit interpersonal responsiveness, such as witnessing the feelings of the therapist, as they tend to invalidate their own perceptions. Most psychodynamic psychotherapists have, however, adapted the approach to suit the needs of various groups of patients and the current economic context (Bergin & Garfield, 1994). These psychodynamic approaches are often integrative, short-term, and focused.

The primacy of individual treatment is not always logical when treating patients who are not psychologically minded, or those who, for other reasons, do not respond to individual verbal psychotherapy. The interpersonal involvement of these patients' significant others, people with whom they live face-to-face, appears more logical and natural. The presence of many individuals in therapeutic settings, such as conjoint or group therapy, also brings a greater variety of ways of intervening, in contrast to individual psychotherapy.

Intense training in open-ended psychotherapy is not without its negative effects. It could make other psychotherapies see more complex than necessary. Working with students and experienced clinicians that are trained exclusively in psychodynamic psychotherapy made me realize how the psychoanalytic attitudes of abstinence and neutrality could make them feel uneasy in interviewing families or a group of patients. Preoccupied with the patient's inner world and attentive to transference phenomena, these clinicians were unresponsive in situations where it would have been more appropriate to respond. If sessions are unstructured and the clinician listens passively, patients and families may leave the interviews confused and sometimes angry, and will not perceive the experience as fruitful.

Cognitive–behavior therapy (CBT) and existential–humanistic therapy share some of the same shortcomings of the psychodynamic approach. In these orientations, it is understood that the way individuals experience a situation is very personal. The same situation may elicit sadness in one person and anxiety or anger in another. Individuals construe their perceptions and develop abstractions about themselves and others, which, in turn, determine their reactions to events. In most individual approaches, the interpersonal world is seen primarily in terms of distorted schemes that are discussed from the patient's perspective.

As the patient's interpersonal environment is not usually observed directly, the therapist may misinterpret the patient's experience, which is very subjective and easily distorted by both parties, compared with the more objective interpersonal reality. Without seing the patient's close relatives, the information gathered about the relational context in which the problem is embedded may be limited and misleading, even though this information is part of the patient's world. The therapist then develops an image about the patient's relatives that has an effect on the therapy. As in the following vignette, incongruities may follow; family interviews can be helpful in providing the therapist with relevant information concerning the patients and their interpersonal environment.

Mrs. Dumont had been in therapy for many years before she asked for help for Jane, her 15-year-old only child. Even though functioning well at work and socially, Mrs. Dumont was perceived by her therapist as having some "borderline" features. Separated twice, she had chaotic love relationships, and felt easily overwhelmed and depressed under stress. Raising an adolescent girl alone had become difficult for Mrs. Dumont. Through her therapist, she referred her daughter for vague feelings of depression and frequent arguments.

Jane was taken in open-ended psychotherapy by a not-well-trained, somewhat depressed therapist who did not see the need to meet with the adolescent's mother at least once, as the mother was also in treatment. The only information concerning the family was provided by Jane. Jane quickly attached to her therapist, idealizing her, which seemed to gratify her therapist's narcissistic need. As the therapist was not ready to receive and contain the adolescent's anger, she failed to tackle the adolescent's splitting and projection of her negative feelings onto her mother and the internal good object onto the therapist. Their collusion was reinforcing the status quo in the family. The adolescent felt better, but after months of treatment was still having open friction with her mother.

The mother–daughter relationship got much worse, with an increase of reciprocal negative behaviors related to Jane's need for greater autonomy. As the mother wanted advice, her therapist suggested that she contact a mental health center. Instead Mrs. Dumont called Jane's therapist repeatedly to complain about her daughter's behavior. The two therapists phoned each other, each siding with their respective client's point of view. The mother's therapist thought Jane should be placed, while Jane's therapist was convinced of the mother's negative role in Jane's acting out behaviors. A social worker was finally involved. Meeting the mother and daughter together provided the social worker with a broader perspective of the problem, which helped a compromise to be reached.

CBT has the limitations of some other directive treatments. Only the more motivated patients will be ready to be actively involved in the program and to follow the therapist's directives, such as doing homework. Narrowing the perspective may foster short-term efficacy at the expense of more adaptive solutions, such as the patient's more appropriate way of living. Recent developments in CBT have led, however, to focusing more on adaptation, as opposed to simple symptom relief. As complement to the traditional cognitive interventions, newer CBT approaches are now developed by a second generation of therapists. While these cognitive therapists were first concerned with empirical methods and practice, they are now developing more elaborate theoretical frameworks based on constructivism to understand and change cognitive processes. Linking cognitive patterns to the concept of attachment and developmental issues also has been an interesting area of investigation (Liotti, 1988). This approach has a strong impact on the teaching and the practice of psychotherapy and is now integrated in conjoint and group therapy.

The existential–humanistic approaches share some advantages and some limitations with the psychodynamic approach. As described by Beutler and Clarkin (1990), in the existential–humanistic experiences, overt symptoms are not considered the direct objective of the experience. They are, rather, the product of unfinished childhood conflicts that are identified in the sessions and dealt with directly by forcing the client to address these conflicts and the accompanying blocked feelings.

Through the existential–humanistic approaches, with supposedly less preconceptions about the patient, one could expect that more people might be reached than by traditional approaches. This has not been the case, however. In the existential–humanistic approach, the patient has to be motivated for awareness and the extensive implication of self could be a deterrent to many. According to Greenberg and colleagues (1994), the existential–humanistic movement is not suited for patients with serious mental illness.

☐ Individual Psychotherapy and the Family

Psychotherapy is a complex phenomenon that may wield great interpersonal power. The effects of individual psychotherapy cannot be acknowledged only within the perspective of the individual in therapy. The focus is on the individual, but the repercussions of the interventions on significant others are sometimes overlooked, as they are not within the focus or responsibility of the therapist. Psychotherapists assume the best interest of their patients, which is assumed to also be the best interest of their significant others.

Even though the patient's improvement usually has a positive effect on their relatives, it is a false assumption that therapeutic benefits for patients will also have beneficial effects on their families in a linear, causal way. This is sometimes the case in the individual treatment of children. The child's desired outcome may be in conflict with that of other family members, for example, a parent or a sibling. The benefits may not have the same significance for the patient's close relatives. For example, an inhibited boy who is afraid and unable to face his overly-strict father should be able, through individual therapy, to express his negative feelings to his father, who may, however, be unwilling or unprepared to accept them.

Since Freud's time, the patient's relatives are often seen as a hindrance to psychotherapy. The relationship between the patient and the therapist, which must be strictly confidential, may partly explain this situation. Relatives are usually kept away and may not be able to question what is going on. The entry of a third person (such as a therapist) in a couple's intimate relationship is not consequence free. These consequences are usually positive, but they may also be negative. It is not uncommon for partners to complain about not being able to obtain information about their mate's problems. The partner who is not in therapy may resist the patient's efforts to change (see chapter 4).

Couples also may come to see their own efforts to work through their marital problems as less feasible. Individual approaches to psychotherapy may sometimes prevent patients from using the resources in their relational environment. In fact, people with emotional problems easily may assume that people who are significant to them cannot be of much help, and an expert, such as a psychotherapist, is needed. The "talking cure" may lead patients to believe they do not have to talk to significant others about their problems, and their partners may share this belief. This may deprive them of natural support.

The treatment of post-traumatic stress disorder is a good illustration.

As more sophisticated individual treatments become available, people who have experienced trauma are advised to look for professional help, even though they may not present symptoms. The support that could be provided from peoples' natural systems can be by-passed, depriving individuals of the opportunity to help each other, to feel competent, and to reinforce their relational environment.

In a literature review of the marital effects of individually-oriented psychotherapy, Hunsley and Lee (1995) found that the long duration of treatment may be partially responsible for some negative marital effects. In most cases, short-term individual psychotherapy had no significant negative effects on the marriage. Studying the reactions of subjects to their mate's psychotherapies, Hatcher and Hatcher (1983) found both positive and negative feelings. Many spouses felt a lack of privacy, because whatever was said between the two in private could be talked about during the sessions. Many spouses reported the patient's self-absorption in psychotherapy, withdrawing from the family, and not listening to their mate during treatment.

The spouse's negative emotional reaction to psychotherapy is best exemplified and most often encountered when the wife is in long-term psychotherapy. The most difficult period is usually when the transference develops, because it may complicate the marital relationship. The spouse may then experience various reactions depending on factors, such as his emotional maturity and the type of relationship he has with his wife.

Individual psychotherapy may be a risk factor for deterioration in chronic marital conflict. In a survey of the literature on deterioration in psychotherapy, Kniskern and Gurman (1985) found significantly more deterioration to marital problems (11%) from individual psychotherapy than in interpersonal treatment involving both spouses (5.6%). The deterioration in these studies included both worsening of the spouse's condition or deterioration of the relationship when the patient improved.

Psychotherapy may be used as a tranquillizer. Individual psychotherapy is sometimes utilized to prevent people from dealing directly with unbearable situations, such as destructive or devaluing relations or preserving a status quo that will make a relational change even more difficult. In a conflict-laden marriage, the husband may encourage his wife to undergo psychotherapy. She may then feel better, while he persists in ignoring her, with a clear conscience. Furthermore, the promise of better well being may create unrealistic expectations of what individual psychotherapy may accomplish. As patients become aware of their problems, they may develop false hope regarding significant others who may not be at the same level of understanding.

Kim, a nurse who retrained as a psychotherapist and had been married for more than 20 years, undertook psychotherapy as part of her psychotherapy training. She also hoped this would improve her marital relationship which had been deteriorating over the years. The partners were distant, each busy in their separate worlds. With the development of the transference, she was very involved in her therapy and constantly talked about the experience. She withdrew from her husband and became more outgoing and secure. This threatened her husband, a quiet and withdrawn individual who became less functional at work. Following his wife's advice that he could profit from this type of experience, he also started psychotherapy. He did not respond well to an unstructured approach and left therapy abruptly, feeling confused about the experience. This increased the distance and tension between the partners, but they did not seem ready to either deal directly with the problem or to separate from each other.

Even though not seen frequently, this situation illustrates some potential negative effects of individual psychotherapy. It is plausible to think that marital deterioration might have been prevented if the couple's interpersonal system had been assessed before engaging the husband in individual psychotherapy. A marital assessment might have found that the marital system was contributing as well to the couple's problems as the individual intrapsychic system.

☐ Working Class and Ethnic Patients

Individual psychotherapy, and psychodynamic psychotherapy in particular, is largely a middle-class phenomenon. Its ethos has been dominated by the ethos of psychoanalysis, which is well suited for the educated middle class professional (Holmes & Lindley, 1989). According to Garfield (1994), who reviewed research on client variables in psychotherapy, the belief system and the outlook on life of the therapist and the patient is another characteristic that influences the psychotherapeutic encounter, and is culturally and class related. In most individual approaches, the psychotherapist is working within a knowledge-based, systematic approach, using distance and reflexive practice (Gartner & Reissman, 1977). The psychodynamic approach, in particular, is often perceived as elitist, with a mystique surrounding the treatment and many rules that could be different from the mode of living of the poor (Holmes & Lindley, 1989). As we will see, this is not usually the case with group and conjoint family therapy.

Having been devised for affluent patients, the use of individual psychotherapy with the lower economic class is not evident. Different

social classes receive different treatment, long-term dynamic psychotherapy being given mainly to middle- and upper-middle-class patients
(Holmes & Lindley, 1989). The typical patient in dynamic psychotherapy is a white, college-educated woman, between the ages of 30 and
40, and living in an upper-middle-class neighborhood (Weber, Solomon,
& Bachrach, 1985).

Whatever their orientation, most psychotherapists prefer to work
individually with young, articulate, and motivated patients, which limits
the applicability of individual psychotherapy. The result is neglect of
the poor, ethnic groups, and older people. Working-class patients are
often not selected because of so called "lack of motivation." Drop-out
rates were much higher among poor patients (only 12% remained in
treatment) as compared to middle-class patients (42%) in one study
reported by Holmes and Lindley (1989).

There is a difference in expectations among social classes in regard
to psychotherapy (Garfield, 1986). Disadvantaged patients expect rapid
symptom relief and a quick solution to their problems. They tend to
see psychological treatment as something the doctor "does" to them
(Garfield, 1986). Lower-class patients frequently expect to receive directives or medication, while upper-middle-class patients may be more
willing to understand their problem and make their own decisions.
This is also true for many ethnic groups. Asian-Americans and Latinos,
for example, prefer a directive therapeutic style (Sue, Zane, & Young,
1994).

When they need help for psychological problems, lower-class patients may resort more to coping techniques, which is far removed
from the underlying assumptions of many individual psychotherapies
(Weber et al., 1985). In both psychodynamic and existential–humanistic approaches, the emphasis and the main therapeutic goal are not
symptom relief but self-exploration and better understanding of self.
Garfield (1994) reported the results of many studies, showing that
patients from the upper classes also remained in treatment longer
than lower-class patients. The criteria set for open-ended psychotherapy
have been more stringent in the past, but because of decreasing funds,
many practitioners are now less selective and have adapted their approach to serve a larger population (Garfield, 1994).

Individual psychotherapy does not always suit cultural minorities.
Minority groups in the United States, including Hispanics, African-
Americans, and Native Americans, use traditional psychotherapy to a
much lesser extent than the rest of the population (Sue et al., 1994).
There has been controversy over the effectiveness of this therapeutic
modality with this population. In a study including 14,000 clients in
17 community mental health centers in the greater Seattle area, Sue

and Zane (1987) reported that half of the ethnic-minority clients failed to return for psychotherapeutic treatment after one session, as compared to a 30% dropout rate among Whites. In a subsequent study, however, this data was not corroborated for Asian-Americans (Sue et al., 1994). Non-White, non-Anglo patients are less frequently accepted for psychotherapy, are more frequently assigned to inexperienced therapists, and more frequently receive medication only (Lefley & Bestman, 1984).

Individual psychotherapy is embedded in a cultural professional work and is sometimes seen as not sufficiently sensitive to patients' culture. As this therapeutic format enhances the individuality of the person, can it be relevant and effective in cultures that promote group interrelationships? As described by Casimir and Morrison (1993), while individual psychotherapy often leads individuals to step back from their culture and question their life and their role, most cultures strongly emphasize the family and the group. Psychotherapy should thus be adjusted accordingly. To Kojima (1984), in cultures that have an inclusive conception of the self, such as the Japanese, if individuals were to draw a line demarcating the representation of the self from the nonself, they would probably include significant others within the region defined as the self.

Anthropological studies (e.g., Dow, 1986) show that symbolic healing is effective, as the mythology is applied to the patient and respects the mythic world and the patient's culture. As a consequence, psychotherapy with ethnic groups or applied to Third World countries may have to be conceptualized, not only as a medical or a psychological act, but also as a sociocultural experience involving significant others. With some ethnic groups, family meetings may be necessary, the emphasis placed as much on the patients' relational environment as on the patients themselves.

Family interviewing, discussion of the problem with the family, and respect of the family hierarchy—characteristics of conjoint therapy—may look more familiar to people living in traditional societies or to ethnic groups. It has been recommended, for example, that the family should be recognized as an integral part of treatment with Asian-Americans (Sue et al., 1994). These authors also suggested the use of group therapy with patients from the same ethnic group.

Summarizing some of the characteristics of poor and minority patients in regard to psychological help, Casimir and Morrison (1993) put these characteristics in contrast with traditional psychotherapy: These patients value efforts toward environmental changes, they want to work in the here-and-now and on concrete issues, they tend to emphasize collective enterprise and interdependence rather than independence and self-actualization. These characteristics may clash with the psychotherapist's assumptions of the necessity for self-disclosure and exploring one's own experience in individual psychotherapy. Sue and colleagues (1994) came to the same conclusion in their summary of various studies about Asian-Americans: They tend to believe that mental health is promoted by avoidance of negative thinking, self-discipline, and refraining from the public expression of feelings.

Freud understood the necessity of increasing the variety of psychotherapy to reach all social classes.

> . . . it is possible to foresee that at some time or other the conscience of society will awake and remind it that the poor man should have just as much right to assistance for his mind as he now has to the life-saving help offered by surgery [. . .] We shall then be faced by the task of adapting our techniques to the new conditions (Freud, 1919, p. 167).

Notwithstanding their shortcomings, all the major individual orientations to psychotherapy have to be preserved and used. To reject psychodynamic understanding, in particular, would entail a great loss for many psychotherapists who often have little training in other psychological perspectives, especially developmental psychology. This modality remains the best instrument for learning about basic phenomena, such as the unconscious and the transference. Moreover, acknowledging these phenomena is essential in the teaching and practice of any type of psychotherapy, including conjoint and group therapy. Next, consider how the interpersonal orientation to psychotherapy offers a large spectrum of therapeutic modalities that can be time effective, cost effective, and less restrictive in dealing with some emotional problems, without necessarily using the individual scheme and the yardstick of the transference. My objective is not a forced conversion to the interpersonal-systemic model, but to suggest this model as a complementary way of conceptualizing and treating emotional problems.

PART

II

THE
INTERPERSONAL

3
CHAPTER

The Interpersonal Orientation

The interpersonal orientation is surprisingly not widely discussed in psychotherapy, as the context favors the intrapsychic dimension. However, group and conjoint family psychotherapy, which are based on the interpersonal orientation, are often brief, structured, and problem-focused; these characteristics particularly suit the current and predicted trend in psychotherapy practice. In interpersonal approaches to psychotherapy, interactional relationships (those that can be observed directly) are emphasized over transferential relationships. The therapist assumes that evaluating and treating the interpersonal dimension of the patient's problem is important to produce enduring and generalized changes (Wachtel & McKinney, 1992).

The advantages of using an interpersonal perspective may not always be clear. The interpersonal orientation is theoretically sound. As we will see in this chapter, the systemic principles such as circular causality which is basic to conjoint therapy, and the emphasis on interpersonal consequences of an individual's behavior, which is the focus of cognitive interpersonal theory, are basic to the interpersonal orientation. The interpersonal dimension can be clinically useful in many ways, including being a way of understanding, as a therapeutic lever or "handle" to promote change, as a process, and as content.

The interpersonal orientation is partly based on the work of Sullivan and other neo-Freudians such as Fromm and Horney. These authors, who were called interpersonal psychoanalysts, contributed to the conception of the person as an interpersonal being and his or her emotional problems as related to faulty interpersonal relations. They were emphasizing the interpersonal to balance Freud's focus on the intra-psychic. Sullivan developed his own theory regarding personality development and treatment. To Sullivan, all aspects of a person had to be seen through the interpersonal perspective. In his book *The Interpersonal Theory of Psychiatry*, Sullivan (1953) sees the personality as basically interpersonal, and the self as above all interpersonal. He defined personality as enduring patterns of interpersonal relations.

To Sullivan, people crave interaction with their human environment for recognition, acceptance, and esteem. The individual has a propensity for interpersonal attachment and for the maintenance of self within one's interpersonal world. The repeated interpersonal experiences between the child and the parents lead to the self-perception of a good and a bad self (Sullivan, 1953). The development and the maintenance of the sense of self is thus made through interactions with others who appraise the individual and the self, and thus, shape one's own appraisals of self and others. Sullivan did not emphasize the importance of fantasy in the elaboration of psychic functioning.

The source of anxiety is also seen by Sullivan (1953) as strictly interpersonal and resulting from interpersonal threats to security and self-esteem. Sullivan perceived psychopathology as resulting from excessive anxiety, which prevents the adequate development of the self. In therapy, he emphasized the exploration of faulty interpersonal patterns and their modification, and the active participation of the therapist, opposing to the abstinence model of psychotherapy.

Even though Sullivan acknowledged internal representation of the self and of other, the self, as defined by Sullivan (1953), may be perceived as a looking glass, in that the individual has no intrapsychic mechanisms and structure to metabolize the images that others put on him or her. These notions have been more thoroughly studied and expanded by object relations psychoanalytic theory, psychoanalytic self-psychology, and infant research. As we will see, some of Sullivan's notions, however, remain basic and have been used by various schools of psychotherapy, especially group and conjoint family therapy. For example, the personality cannot be understood without the context of interpersonal relations, and interpersonal transactions are based on continuous negotiation of complementary needs among participants.

☐ Neglect of the Interpersonal

If we include private practice, most of the mental health resources focus on individual treatment that could be done at the expense of other important participants in the mental health system, such as the family. One looks to the singularities of the patient's past or the particularities of his or her molecular biology to explain maladaptive behavior. What is going on interpersonally may be seen only as the result of the contributions of the individuals involved, and not emerging from their particular interaction. Treating a psychiatric or a psychological problem as if it exists only in the individual's thoughts or brain chemicals ignores important aspects of human functioning. The interpersonal context of emotional disorders deserves careful attention.

The context favors individual psychotherapy. The individualistic paradigm, the predominant ideology, is so omnipresent that clinicians in their day-to-day practice usually remain within the individual sphere. The interpersonal approach involving groups of patients or families is not often used, since therapeutic modalities involving more than one individual are often seen as second rate. The patient may be referred for these modalities when there is nobody available or willing to do individual therapy. Even clinicians' offices are usually built to see only a few individuals at a time.

In the treatment of emotional problems, intervention is often done by a team of mental health workers whose leader is usually a psychiatrist. He or she often gets involved in the individual part of the treatment and delegates the other aspects of the problem to another team member. Because the psychiatrist is often seen as the most knowledgeable person of the team by patients and their families, the intervention (often pharmacotherapy) is perceived as central while the other treatments are perceived as secondary. Along the same lines, when the medical doctor does not value, for example, family or group involvement, the quality of these interventions can decrease. This negative attitude may influence how the other professionals will get involved. When psychiatrists are comfortable with the interpersonal-systemic perspective, cooperating with those who see the patients' families is easier.

Commenting on the importance of integrating various perspectives in psychotherapy, Norcross and Newman (1992) argue that the patient may behave quite differently in different contexts and that individual psychotherapy may not allow the therapist to observe the patient interacting with anyone other than the therapist. Some traits may not become readily apparent in individual treatment while, in group and conjoint family therapy, the recapitulative interpersonal patterns are evoked automatically as well as the feared responses of the others.

☐ Systemic Model and the Interpersonal

A purely individual psychology cannot account for a large proportion of human behavior. A supraindividual focus is needed to reach a
global view of complex phenomena, such as psychiatric illness, so as
to seize the illness in its various components and to link diverging
perspectives. A supraindividual interdependent perspective emphasizes,
for example, that health and illness are aspects of larger systems such
as the family, and are not completely located within the individual.
This does not contradict the importance of biology in mental illness;
the mentally ill person affects and is affected by his family.

This supraindividual framework, a central structure in the various
approaches used in mental health, has been given various names: the
systemic model, the biopsychosocial model, and the ecological model.
Within this framework, the intrapsychic and the interpersonal, have
to be incorporated as parts of an hierarchically-organized and integrated whole. The theoretical and clinical knowledge to go beyond
the psychologies related to the individual are in place, but the main
orientations in psychotherapy have traditionally given primacy to the
individual approach, even though they acknowledge a larger theoretical scheme for understanding the individual.

For diagnostic or therapeutic purposes, it is often less convenient
for clinicians to take into consideration the patients' interpersonal-
systemic context, that is, the world in which they live. Having to deal
with more than one individual increases the complexity, brings uncertainty and confusion, and often means more work for already over-
worked clinicians. The clinician who uses a systemic framework or
another supraindividual model is, however, better placed to choose
the approach that will optimally help the patient, be it seeing the
patient alone, with one or many persons close to him, in a group, or
simply meeting people who are part of the patient's network without
seeing the patient.

In his general systems theory, von Bertalanffy (1968), a biologist,
adapted the organismic principle to other disciplines; it states that
organisms are structured and organized. Nowadays, systemic understanding does not create much of a problem, as this notion is com-
monly used to explain various phenomena, such as the global economy
and ecological disasters. Applied to the interpersonal field of psychotherapy, the general system theory implies that:

1. Human systems are organized hierarchically. These systems are open
   and in interaction. If the person is considered an open system,
   finding alternatives beyond the individual, and beyond a individual

view of psychotherapy, may counteract the latent pessimism toward chronic mental illness. Exploration and use of outside forces, such as the interpersonal field of the patient, may also help prevent burnout and, using Sutherland's (1981) words, decrease the "unrealistic expectations of what intrapsychic change alone might achieve" (p. 125).

2. New properties emerge from systems when they reach a certain level of organization. These properties cannot be grasped through the analytic study of the parts, because of the notion of nonsummativity. For example, the individual evaluation of patients abstracted from their intersubjective interpersonal context does not allow a full understanding of the complex reality of these patients. Similarly, the individual assessment or treatment of all the members of a family or a group does not give an adequate idea of that family's or group's functioning (see the vignettes in which all the family members were in individual psychotherapy, in chapters 2 and 4).

3. Human systems function through the circularity of their interactions, which form a circular loop. This circular functioning is regulated by feedback, which is the basis of circular causality.

Circular causality is fundamental to some interpersonal approaches to psychotherapy, such as conjoint family therapy; it shows its importance, for example, in that communication problems between two individuals may be seen as being related to a difference of perception in a circular situation. In the sequence of behaviors in a spousal argument, each spouse may have a linear view of the causality of the problem and use pathological attribution as a way to prevent self-blame. The behavior of one of the two individuals can be unilaterally defined as the cause of the other's behavior, which would then be seen as the effect. On the one hand, the wife nags her husband because she may believe that he withdraws from her and does not seem to be interested in her; on the other hand, the husband keeps his distance because he may think that his wife is the cause of his withdrawal as she nags him continuously. In circular thinking, they are part of a circular loop; the withdrawal of one leads to the other's criticisms and vice versa.

As Kiesler (1982) states, it is "an arbitrary slicing of reality" (p. 9) to perceive the behavior of one participant of a dyad as the cause and the reaction of the other as the effect. The other's prior and simultaneous input into the behavior of the first person is, then, not taken into account. The therapist who takes an interpersonal-systemic approach and sees both participants together is in a better position to see their biases and prevent linear thinking (see the case of Mr. Wilson that follows). The individual therapist who sees only one spouse may tend to confirm that spouse's perception of the problem and could misunderstand the dynamics involved.

This nonlinear approach decreases the chance of using reductionism and determinism, and encourages the utilization of interpersonal and systemic properties. In a circular causality scheme, the focus on one cause is prevented and the notion of "depth" in therapy loses its mystique. It should be noted, however, to the credit of modern psychodynamic psychotherapists, that the concept of circular causality is now taken into account in dynamic psychotherapy.

This circular loop may also be used to explain change. Many psychotherapeutic approaches are based on the assumption that if the individual's intrapsychic world is changed, the interpersonal field will also change. Other approaches emphasize the other end of the loop: Changing the intersubjective interpersonal environment will lead to the modification of the individual and the intrapsychic. Ideally, psychotherapy should aim to change both ends of the loop simultaneously.

The importance of circular loops in the interpersonal-systemic perspective is manifested by the complementarity existing in relations and roles. As the relationship between two people develops and the system they form evolves, their behavior becomes reduntant, complementary, and leads to recursive loops. This is well evidenced in studies of infants that show that very early on infants and their caretakers engage each other in a circular manner—since they are part of a system.

The complementarity and recursivity of relationships is one factor that is often seen in disturbed relationships (again, see the case of Mr. Wilson below or the case of Mrs. Clark, in chapter 6). The classic example of the wife who nags and the husband who withdraws mentioned before is another illustration. The wife may be seen as the pursuer who complains that her partner is not available enough, while the husband uses this pursuing as the reason to keep an emotional distance. As work with marital partners may show, as soon as the pursuer stops pursuing, the distancer may react and become the pursuer while the former pursuer may become the distancer, arguing that "it is too late." In this case, each partner seems to need emotional distance. Each provides some flaws that will justify the other's need to remain emotionally distant. The persistence of these interpersonal-systemic patterns often means a collusion between the two that can be better dealt with by involving both partners in the treatment.

Human systems, however, are complex and the complementarity between, for example, the abuser and the abused cannot be reduced to a circular causality. Circularity emphasizes reciprocity and complementarity in human relations at the expense of power, hierarchy, and responsibility. The invalidation of power could be a consequence of adopting the notion of circular causality in interpersonal-systemic relations as an exclusive causal model.

Goldner (1991) argues that the concept of circularity could then lead to either a shared responsibility between members of a human system or an absence of responsibility. The abused would be responsible for the abuser's action and vice versa, as if they both had equal power in the relationship. Various social organizations, in particular feminists, have strongly reacted against this systemic position, taking into account the inequality of power in society and families. The family treatment of violence, for example, cannot ignore this inequality and other social conditions (Goldner, 1991). The abuser's responsibility must be clearly acknowledged.

☐ Interpersonal Consequences of Behavior

Social psychologists and cognitive–behavioral researchers have given scientific status to the interpersonal approach. From Sullivan's (1953) idea that psychopathology originates in the interpersonal matrix, these authors consider that the same psychopathology comes out in the interpersonal sphere (Wachtel, 1987). The notion of current interpersonal processes is then crucial in human problems and their resolutions. Consequently, according to these authors, one way of dealing with problems interpersonally is to put emphasis on the interpersonal consequences that the patient produces in others, usually unintentionally. In disturbed interpersonal relationships, these consequences are usually aversive.

Wachtel (1987; Wachtel & McKinney, 1992) argues that interpersonal malfunctioning is often maintained through a circular loop. Maladaptive behavior may have originated in early childhood, and may be based in early wishes that are still the motivational force, leading patients to perpetuate the problem by the choices they make and by the way they live. In return, their behavior provokes reactions in the people with whom they interact, which entrenches the beliefs and perpetuate the problem.

Through a "self-fulfilling prophecy" (Wachtel & McKinney, 1992, p. 355), the patient who expects rejection may behave in an disengaged manner, eliciting a rejecting response from the other, which in turn, increases their feeling of rejection. Wachtel and Mckinney explain that obsessive patients present themselves as rational and guarded, which may raise feelings of frustration and boredom in others and lead them to avoid these patients, contributing to the negative behavior of the obsessive. To understand the foundation of cognitive–interpersonal theory, refer to the *Handbook of Interpersonal Psychotherapy*, edited by Anchin and Kiesler (1982).

The interpersonal setting provided by conjoint family or group therapy is particularly suited to reveal the interpersonal consequences of behavior. The group or family therapeutic environment seems to be a more natural place to experiment compared to long-term psychodynamic psychotherapy, where the therapist may be perceived as an authority figure for a long time. Even though it is not used exclusively in group and conjoint family therapy, the interpersonal dimension characterizes these two therapeutic modalities. The interpersonal perspective is an essential element of conjoint family therapy and contributes more to its specificity than any other component, including systems theory. However, because of the omnipresence of systems theory, even in conjoint family therapy, the interpersonal dimension is not widely discussed.

☐ Interpersonal Orientation and Individual Psychotherapy

The interpersonal perspective is an important component of the interpersonal psychotherapy (IPT). IPT will not be described at length, as the focus of this book is on interpersonal interventions involving families and groups. In brief, IPT is a problem-centered, time-limited individual therapy originally developed by Klerman and his collaborators (1984) for the treatment of depression. The goal of IPT is not to change one's personality, but rather to master social roles and adapt to interpersonal situations linked to the onset of symptoms.

IPT has been developed from a conceptualization of depression that emphasizes the interpersonal field. This therapeutic modality is based on previous empirical studies that found that the onset of depression in women is often related to interpersonal stresses, especially marital friction. Assuming that depression is related to the disruption of the patient's interpersonal context, the therapist aims at improving that context (see Weissman & Paykel, 1994; see also chapter 4).

As described by Cornes and Frank (1996), problems are defined and examined in terms of how disturbed interpersonal relationships and social events contribute to the depressive symptoms. A systematic review of the patient's relationships with significant others is made with special attention to life-cycle changes and their attendant role transitions, and role disputes, to loss experiences and interpersonal skill deficits. Then, one of these problem areas is focused on, which should then lead to better control of social life and resolution of interpersonal conflicts (Cornes & Frank 1996).

IPT is face-to-face therapy. As the consequences of the depressed persons' behavior on others are emphasized, their self-defeating style in their relationship with the therapist is closely scrutinized and worked through (Klerman et al., 1984). Patients develop and test strategies to deal with their day-to-day interpersonal context. The therapist does not respond in a complementary fashion to the usual responses the patient evokes in others. He or she plays an active role, such as prescribing experiences to evoke the self-defeating patterns of the patient. There is also an educational component to IPT, as information is given about depression and its causes.

Any individual psychotherapy has some interpersonal components. CBT, in particular, is very sensitive to the interpersonal environment, context, and reinforcers. Beck (Alford, & Beck, 1997) insists on the importance of the interpersonal environment in influencing cognition. Priority is given to the interpersonal relationship between the therapist and the patient, and is the primary ground to improve the patient's interpersonal skills. The therapist is active and has a structured role. The CBT model may be used within a variety of interpersonal formats such as conjoint and group therapy. In CBT as well as in IPT, the focus is on the individual's perspective, the systemic notion of emergence and circularity, which is always present when two individuals form a system, is not necessarily taken into account. The systemic perspective must be added to explain patterned and complementary behavior.

☐ A Level of Understanding

Interpersonal understanding is discussed in various parts of this book. There are many ways to promote interpersonal understanding. For example, the therapist may present the problem within an interpersonal perspective and analyze it in interpersonal terms even though the problem may seem to be more clearly related to another dimension such as the intrapsychic. Nichols (1988) reports the case of a therapist who asks a man, who finds his wife boring, to explain how he manages to elicit this type of response from his wife.

Even defense mechanisms, usually seen as an intrapsychic phenomenon, have an interpersonal component. Wachtel and Wachtel (1986) present defense mechanisms as interpersonal maneuvers to transfer anxiety when there is a great deal of tension and no solution. These authors describe how in projective identification, for example, feelings and other disavowed aspects of self may be split and attributed to various family members who may feel forced to think and behave in a way congruent with this projection. In dealing with a wish that he or she is trying to repress, an individual may try to prevent relatives from evoking this forbidden wish. The success of these maneuvers will depend upon the individual's ascendancy over the people involved and their degree of collusion with the defense (Wachtel & Wachtel, 1986). Reframing from the personal to the interpersonal fosters the use of the interpersonal perspective as the level for change.

☐ A Therapeutic Lever

The interpersonal dimension, not the biological or the social, is the healing power in interpersonal psychotherapies. The interpersonal is at the heart of their therapeutic goal, which includes identifying maladaptive interpersonal patterns and restoring mutually satisfying interpersonal relationships. Conjoint family and group therapy are effective through their interpersonal characteristics, which create a medium for change.

Both conjoint and group therapy rely on interpersonal relationships to resolve problems. From an interpersonal theoretical scheme, an approach to therapy is used that emphasizes the importance of the others and of relations as a therapeutic lever to learn from one another and to correct relationship disturbances (Yalom, 1995). To work at the interpersonal level means that all participants must contribute to the task. Their here-and-now interpersonal interventions are potent agents of change, which do not exclude the use of historical material at times.

Group or family members are present as "real objects," usually both as helpers and helpees, and their interactions are used as a therapeutic lever. The confrontation with "real" objects can then decrease the influence of internal objects and maximize change often in a better way than what a therapist can do alone with the patient. The therapist does not usually present formal teaching nor provide all the answers, but is still fairly active to instill a therapeutic atmosphere and to promote interactions between members.

> In spite of the therapist's interpretation of her understanding of the situation, marital therapy had been going on for months without much change in the couple's mutually aversive behavior. Mr. Wilson's egocentric and irresponsible behavior had led him many times in the past to individual therapy, to no avail. In marital therapy, however, it became evident that some of his reprehensible behavior was closely related to

his wife's attitudes and were ways to get back at her. Their behavior had become patterned, complementary, and recursive.

Mr. Wilson was chronically late and typically uninvolved with his child and the family chores. With good reason, his wife saw him as her "second child" but so far she had not been able to see her own contribution to their problems, as spelled out many times by the therapist. She was trying to totally control her husband, and corrected anything he tried to do. Regardless of Mr. Wilson feeling more depressed or less depressed, his wife's attitudes remained the same. She could not trust him, but it was found that she had developed that attitude toward men long before they met.

What triggered a change in the marital relationship is difficult to delineate, but the therapist reported a series of sessions that she felt had been pivotal. Within an atmosphere of empathy and firmness, Mr. Wilson had finally acknowledged the inappropriateness of some of his behavior. In the following session, he surprisingly expressed some authentic feelings and concerns for his wife, He accurately recognized her painful feelings, remained attuned to them, and made some concrete suggestions for the two of them to spend more time together. Mrs. Wilson remained skeptical, and did not see any change in her husband's attitudes, which were obvious to the therapist.

For the first time, with the therapist's support, Mr. Wilson did not give up and persisted in his wish to bring about a change. In the here-and-now of the interactions between the two partners, the wife finally realized her inappropriate defensiveness. Being softened by her husband's empathic attitudes, in tears she voiced her pain and talked about her role in maintaining some of their problems. They left the session feeling better, and she was a bit more convinced of his good intentions and of his capacity to listen to her own painful feelings.

The intervention made evident that a key component of this man's emotional problems were related to his interpersonal system, that is, his relationship to his wife. It was logical to use this interpersonal system as a therapeutic lever to change his, as well as his wife's, beliefs about his capacity for change. The example illustrates the power of interpersonal consequences of behavior, as discussed above. The wife's attitude was a reinforcing agent for maintaining her husband's inappropriate behavior. More importantly, the therapist added the systemic perspective to the interpersonal. Each spouse's dysfunctional behavior was reinforcing that of the other. Seeing the spouses together, the therapist was in a better position to see their biases and the complementarity of their behavior, and to prevent linear thinking. The therapist structured the intervention accordingly. They slowly learned to address their marital problems in a more direct and constructive way.

In therapy, a member may validate another member's position or, as in the case of Mr. Wilson, participate in breaking down the other's idiosyncratic attitudes or distorted perceptions of self and others. This lack of confirmation leads to a shift from a subjective to an externally-validated perception. The problem is staged and seen by an audience (the family, the group, the therapist). It is thus submitted to analysis and may become the focus of the others' feedback. Participants may also learn a lot about what to do just by observing the therapist inter-acting with a difficult member. This is illustrated in the case of Mr. Harris (see chapter 7) when the therapist did some individual psy-chotherapy in presence of Mr. Harris' wife.

Affective sharing is also a component of therapeutic interpersonal settings and a strong lever. The expression of positive feelings, such as empathy and support by one member to another, may be more effec-tive than the therapist's support. The patients' fear of the interper-sonal consequences of their behavior such as rejection or disapproval of their affective disclosure may finally be perceived as irrational, as the feared response is not elicited. The case of Ann in Chapter 5 illus-trates this in group therapy.

☐ A Process and a Content

The interpersonal psychotherapist does not focus on the behavior per se, as in classical behavior therapy, but rather on human interactions and processes. Interpersonal processes and interaction sequences are thus important elements in the interpersonal approach. These ele-ments, which bind the members to each other, may be the material used to produce change by those taking a behavioral and a communi-cation approach to working with interactions (Jacobson & Addis, 1993). A therapist can work on improving communications, for example, by promoting interactions and then using feedback to clarify verbal and nonverbal exchanges.

An interpersonal orientation does not mean that the approach is simply interactional and ahistorical, based on overt behavior and not on content. The interpersonal orientation allows to take other levels of human functioning into consideration, since interactions and pro-cesses also instill content and affects, and specifically the intersubjectivity (the shared intrapsychic experience) present in any human interaction (Stolorow & Atwood, 1992). Intersubjectivity is an important content in interpersonal intervention. Members share their subjective life and what results from their intersubjective influence (common meanings) becomes the locus of study. This is shown in the case of the daughter and her mother in chapter 1.

In fact, group and conjoint family therapy often moves back and forth between process and content. How the content is discussed and how the members behave and react are observed to help them see how they may be ineffective in dealing with some emotional content. Any psychotherapeutic orientation dealing with content may be used within an interpersonal scheme, as much as the therapist sees the interplay between process, content, and affect, and uses observation and feedback. The psychodynamic approach, in particular, has been used extensively in group and conjoint family therapy. The pathological use of a defense mechanism, such as a projection and the underlying affect (the content), may be worked on in the presence of other members who act as observers that can support and bring out the interpersonal consequences of the projection and its re-appropriation (the process).

☐ Cotherapy

Cotherapy is particularly useful and well-suited to group and conjoint family therapy. Group and conjoint therapy are complex and require a lot of work from the therapist. On the one hand, the number of verbal and nonverbal exchanges taking place in these interpersonal approaches is huge and better assimilated by two therapists. In addition, group and family therapists experience various intense and quickly shifting emotional reactions that may disturb their perceptions and may be better dealt with by two therapists.

Cotherapy usually helps maintain a distance between therapists and participants and an appropriate therapeutic stance in dealing with difficult issues related, for example, to members' alternating idealization and devaluation of the therapists. Sharing the hardship of therapy before or after each session can ease the therapist's role. A team of therapists can more easily master the participants' resistance while preserving the therapeutic alliance.

Besides facilitating understanding and mutual support between the therapists, cotherapy increases ways of intervening. Flexibility and creativity, essential therapist skills in interpersonal interventions (Bagarozzi, 1996), are promoted by cotherapy. For example, adapting methods and techniques, a common occurrence in interpersonal therapy, is easier when cotherapy is used. Cotherapists can split roles—one therapist can be more active, the other can be more supportive. They can, as well, validate each other's feedback. In addition, showing authenticity and mutual respect to each other, cotherapists can model for the other group members conflict resolution and adaptation. Finally, cotherapy is also useful for training in group and conjoint family therapy.

☐ **Limitations**

The interpersonal orientation cannot usually be used as a single model. Conjoint and group therapy are often not a sufficient approach to assess intrapsychic problems and to treat severe psychiatric illnesses. First of all, compared to individual therapy, they do not provide as much confidentiality. Patients are often unwilling to discuss some private issues concerning themselves, such as abuse, suicidal ideations, and forbidden impulses, in the presence of family or group therapy members. The fear of exposure is greatly increased in conjoint and group sessions.

As explained by Feldman (1992), the limited amount of time available to each member in group and sometimes in conjoint family therapy may prevent in-depth exploration. To reach that goal, individual assessment of the patient is usually necessary. In addition, interpersonal change processes alone are sometimes insufficient to reduce or eliminate the problem, and individual sessions may be needed. The importance of individual sessions is also shown by the fact that adding individual sessions to a group intervention may help decrease dropout rates (Yalom, 1995; see also the concept of sequential therapies discussed in chapter 8).

In discussing treatment mode and format, Beutler and Clarkin (1990) argue that the patient role definition and role complementarity are not as clear and cannot be as easily expected in the family and group format when compared to individual therapy. This may create resistance among group or family members and limit the use of these modalities.

As discussed by Garfield (1994), all experienced clinicians know that patients and their significant others usually hold beliefs about the problem at hand and have their own preferences for treatment, and that these greatly influence the treatment that will be recommended. Usually patients and their families have strong preference for individual treatment (Beutler & Clarkin, 1990). The prevailing biological model can make the involvement of the patient's significant others more difficult. They may not see their contribution to the illness, and may tend to shift responsibility to the patient and to professionals, refusing to be actively involved in the treatment.

Since conjoint therapy depends on compliance, strategies may have to be used to involve reluctant members. Patients' significant others, who do not see their role or their involvement in the problems presented, may be invited to come for a short period of time, being told that their presence is essential to better understand the patient (in some cases, the treatment may not proceed without the presence of the patient's significant others). The therapist's hidden agenda may then be to sensitize them to their role in the problem—whether positive or negative. Reluctant members may later acknowledge their influence and become active participants of the process of change. However, if these people remain unable to see their influence, they may still be involved as "cotherapists."

Group therapy is contraindicated for a number of conditions (see Leszcz, 1996), which limit its application, such as acutely-psychotic patients who cannot tolerate too much stimulation and cannot focus on the group process, paranoid patients, suicidal patients, violent patients, and many patients with character disorders. These contraindications are, however, relative, as almost all patients can be suited for some specific type of group. This is the same for conjoint family therapy, to the point that the family therapy literature rarely mentions contraindications. As we will see, conjoint family therapy is not one approach, it is many. The variation in goals and populations determines the type of problems suited for a given approach and its contraindications (Nichols & Schwartz, 1998).

Group and conjoint family therapy is an undertaking that is more emotionally demanding compared to individual psychotherapy. This may be a deterrent to many who, in addition, may not be paid better for the extra work. Finally, conjoint and group therapy are more difficult to organize. The absence of one member may jeopardize the session or the whole intervention. All these factors may help explain why most clinicians are still reluctant to use conjoint and group therapy as part of their work. Some of these limitations may contribute to make the combination of group and conjoint family therapy to other psychotherapy formats more important (see chapter 8).

In the following chapters, conjoint family and group therapy will be discussed in more details. These psychotherapeutic modalities could lend themselves to the short-term interventions that are now the backbone of mental health programs. Group and conjoint family therapy, however, runs countercurrent to social and health policies, which often deemphasize solidarity and mutual aid provided by people close to the patient or those sharing the same condition.

4
CHAPTER

Conjoint Therapy

Conjoint family therapy is a major force in the mental health field and is taught in all the major health and mental health disciplines. Various components of conjoint therapy will now be reviewed and this interpersonal-systemic approach will be discussed as it applies to resistance in psychotherapy and to depression.

☐ Definition

Conjoint family therapy is multi-faceted and covers a wide range of clinical approaches. On the one hand, it is a conceptual paradigm, sustained by interpersonal and systems theories, departing from traditional clinical approaches to psychiatry, and focusing on relationships between people. On the other hand, conjoint family therapy is a search for realistic and practical ways to tackle human problems and relieve human suffering. However, family therapy, is mostly known as a differentiated, autonomous profession, a specific approach with a set of methods and techniques.

Conjoint family therapy is not necessarily understood as treating the whole family directly, but rather understanding the role that significant others play in the problem and, if needed, involving them in the treatment. The patients' significant others are usually part of the nuclear or extended family. For patients living outside their family, this could be a heterosexual or homosexual partner, a close friend, a fellow tenant, or even the head of the group home where the patient lives. This approach relates more to the way of conceptualizing and tackling problems, rather than to the number of people present in the session. As there are various forms of committed relationships, the term "family therapy" may be seen as a misnomer. The use of the term "conjoint therapy" may be more appropriate.

Conjoint therapy is also what is usually called systemic therapy. In order to understand the complexity of the patients's lives, systemic therapy emphasizes the understanding of relationships in the context of their ecosystems. However, to emphasize the interpersonal as much as the systemic, the term conjoint therapy will be used in this book.

In searching for practical ways to tackle human problems, conjoint therapy may vary tremendously in the goals and modalities of application, depending on factors such as the presenting problem and the age of the index patient. Educating and counseling can be done in conjoint therapy as well as using specific methods and techniques. The therapist's position will vary accordingly from being a teacher and a consultant, to being a facilitator or someone who does not have the answers. Conjoint therapy also may be used within various psychotherapeutic orientations.

☐ Rationale

Within the model conceptualizing the individual as part of an interpersonal system of intimate relationships, involving significant others in the assessment and treatment appears both natural and logical. Meeting the patient's family or significant others should, whenever possible, be part of the diagnostic assessment. No description of the patient's relational environment is as powerful as seeing and experiencing the interaction between the patient and this environment.

Many psychiatrists and psychologists believe that they do not have to be directly involved with the patient's family and see this work as more suitable for social workers. The busy clinician or the treating team may not take the time to sit with the partner or the family and contextualize the problematic behavior de visu. If the couple or the family is assessed, however, the problematic behavior may become less strange and may even be seen as a necessary consequence of the family functioning. In addition, the wealth of information helps assess family resources, develop a proper treatment plan, and build the confidence and cooperation of the family.

The case of Tim, a 17-year-old adolescent referred by his mother for rebellious behavior at home, illustrates how a family screening may quickly reveal that the identified patient may paradoxically be the family member who functions the best. Tim was doing quite well both at school and socially. During the family interview, his rebellious behavior targeted toward his overcontrolling stepfather appeared to be a sane and adaptive response to an intolerable family situation. Since the stepfather had moved in one year earlier, he had exerted total control over the family. Tim's mother felt drained from her previous marital relationship, and saw her new boyfriend as a savior. She then let him take over the family functioning. The couple bought a house, which the mother saw as security she had never had before.

The stepfather became tyrannical towards the mother and Tim, while Mary, the 15-year-old daughter, was spared. The mother was unable to defend herself and became depressed, while Tim expressed the family's and his own distress by opposing the unreasonable rules imposed by his stepfather. The exclusive use of individual interviews probably would have led the clinician to the same conclusion about the adolescent's behavior, but the amount of information about the family system, the tension that emerged out of the family, and each family member's reaction to it in particular, would not have been observed. The family evaluation showed that the family system was closed and a prisoner of itself, while the symptom was an attempt to reopen it. Taking the family context into consideration, Tim's oppositional behavior became more easily understandable.

The interviewer, an experienced clinician with no formal training in conjoint therapy, quickly stepped in to modulate the expression of strong negative feelings. He was able to empathize with all family members, including the stepfather who had experienced hard times before joining the family, and to gain their cooperation. This is difficult to do when individual therapy is chosen without seeing the patient's relatives. Based on this systemic understanding, the situation necessitated a specific intervention logically involving more than the index patient.

This family intervention meant that the clinician had confidence on the family's resources to deal with the problem. He intended to empower the adolescent's natural system, a mechanism discussed further below. The interviewer was actively structuring the session, and placed himself within an interpersonal-systemic perspective.

For a better-informed diagnosis, the family has to be taken into account, whichever *DSM-IV* axis (1-11) is considered. More accurate information can be obtained by interviewing the patient's family. The *Diagnostic and Statistical Manual of the American Psychiatric Association* (DSM) classification of mental disorders, with its primary focus on the individual, has been seen, however, as inadequate for family-oriented clinicians because it has nothing to do with family assessment. Marital and family problems have been relegated to a section called the V codes (Conditions not Attributed to a Mental Disorder that Are a Focus of Attention or Treatment) and unfortunately, no criteria have been defined for the V codes.

The family is also important in mental health prevention. Family-based preventive interventions may be an alternative to individual- and school-based programs that promote only individual skills. This has been shown, in particular, in working with youth at risk for behavior problems such as delinquency and drug use (Hogue & Liddle, 1999). Ecological research strongly supports the notion that there is better family functioning and better child development when clinicians invest in families, and when family-oriented care is used by health care providers (Bronfenbrenner, 1986).

Unlike many psychotherapists working with individuals who may perceive the interests and worries of the patient's family as a hindrance, the family-oriented clinician welcomes the family and uses it as an asset. Conjoint therapy implies empowering the patient's natural system as a force available in the interpersonal field and assumes there is usually something essentially good about that system. Empowering significant others means fostering reliance on their own resources and establishing a partnership with them. A unique asset in using the collectivity of significant others as helpers is the fact that this group is the same both inside and outside of the therapeutic setting.

Conjoint therapy, however, does not replace the individual approach, which is necessary for the evaluation and usually for at least part of the treatment of most emotional problems. Individual treatment should not impede, however, people's capacity to solve their problems. The treatment of children with functional problems illustrates well this statement. If a psychotherapist sees the child alone, the opportunity to empower the parents in their capacity to solve their parental problems may be missed. Whenever feasible, helping the parents and their problematic child to find their own solutions may be a better alternative. This stance often goes against the professionalization of mental health services that have taken over what was formerly done by lay people.

The family-oriented therapist's position could be compared to the general practitioner's at the time that treatment was home-based. The family doctor knew the family and took family factors into account in prescribing treatment. As medicine became specialized and hospital care developed, the family was often neglected as the unit of care. In investigating 732 American families, Murata and Kane (1987) made that neglect evident. In only 16.7% of the families they studied did parents use the same primary care physician. Even though family practice is more common in the community than it was 15 years ago, it is still rare that the clinician inquires about the well-being of the patient's offspring.

☐ **Evolution**

Conjoint therapy as a discipline is in a state of transformation. At the time of the formation of schools of family therapy in the 60s and the 70s, systems purists were revering systems theory and defending the orthodoxy of the systemic approach to counterbalance the influence of psychoanalysis. These pioneers were giving a predominant place to techniques which is now sometimes called "technolatry." In strategic family therapy (Haley, 1976), for example, the therapist is giving directives that the family has to follow for symptom removal; if the family is found to be resistant to these directives, the therapist devises paradoxical injunctions such as symptom prescription to recoup the power and outwit the family. Paradoxical techniques were sometimes used indiscriminately, which helped keep clinicians away from conjoint therapy. These systemic techniques have their place in the therapist's choice of methods but must be used with circumspection.

Systems theory is only a methodology, a scheme to understand complex phenomena, a macroscope, and cannot be used alone as therapeutic substrate. This theory was humanized, taking into account a person's subjectivity, particularly by Ackerman (1958) as early as the 40s and the 50s. A psychoanalyst, Ackerman used the family interview format to deal with children and their parents. In 1958, he wrote the first book on family therapy, articulating system theory and psychodynamic concepts.

The discipline of conjoint therapy is currently influenced by the postmodernist movement that has emerged in arts and in social sciences. It questions rationality and replaces it with pluralism and subjectivity. The approach has moved from focusing on objectivation of the family to a constructivist position that allows a better consideration of the individual and his subjectivity. Some pioneers' models (i.e., structural, strategic) which were based on norms and on the illusion to develop powerful techniques are now being questioned. The subjectivity of the individual is now used to replace Watzlawick's notion of the mind as a black box too complex to consider in therapy (Watzlawick, Beavin, & Jackson, 1967). The social constructionist view, in particular, which focuses on ways human groups collectively construct meanings and narratives (Gergen, 1992) underlies many new family approaches.

As described by Nichols and Schwartz (1998), the role of the therapist as being responsible for change has been supplanted by the role of constructing a new reality with the family and the therapist being a collaborator. The therapist shows interest and curiosity but, whenever possible, takes the position of "not knowing." This move forces the participant members to be their own experts and to use their own resources. Therapists, however, remain in control of the therapeutic process. They make sure the atmosphere is therapeutic, keep the focus on one theme at a time, and allow each participant to present his or her own perspective safely.

As reported by Shields and colleagues (1994), conjoint therapy, understood as a systemic therapy, unfortunately remains a deterrent to many clinicians. The systemic model has significantly increased the amount of knowledge related to mental health and mental illness, bringing new perspectives whose links to the actual work with families are not always evident. Because of the malleability of its framework, conjoint therapy is constantly changing, and more than any other therapeutic modality, it is easily influenced by any new and fashionable movement of the mental health industry, which could be confusing for the clinician. Finally, some clinicians still believe that conjoint therapy is primarily the application of a series of behavioral techniques by insensitive therapists who think it is necessary to confront all painful emotions.

☐ Indications

According to Combrinck-Graham (1996), for someone who thinks in systemic-interpersonal terms, the question is not whether the patient's significant others should be involved or not, but whom to involve and when. A conjoint approach is particularly indicated when the conditions required for the use of a therapeutic intervention (i.e., a patient presents problems, suffers from them, and requests help) are not present with only one person but are spread instead among many individuals, most often among family members. A nonpsychotic individual, for example, may present symptoms but deny their existence or attribute them to another person, while the people who live with the individual suffer or worry. This is frequent with patients presenting a personality disorder.

In their discussion of treatment selection, Beutler and Clarkin (1990) state that conjoint therapy is both logical and more effective with patients in a position of dependence such as children and older people. The patient is then accompanied by somebody else, be it a parent or a spouse, who has to wait while the patient is seen. The patient's level of separation–individuation from his family is also a good criteria for using conjoint therapy. Physical separation is not an exclusion criteria, though, as patients still may be emotionally involved in a pathological way with their family. Conjoint (or group) treatment also may be of help in weaning dependent patients who are in need of constant attention from their therapist when they are away from individual treatment.

Conjoint intervention can be carried out with a large number of individuals who do not have the ability to undertake traditional psychotherapy (see chapter 3). In addition, conjoint therapy can be used with any social class or level of education. The work of Minuchin with families of the slums (Minuchin, Montalvo, Guerney, Rosman, & Shumer, 1967) and later with more sophisticated families (Minuchin, 1974) is a good example of this.

It is not infrequent that all family members are seen simultaneously in individual psychotherapy. This situation, even though sometimes necessary, often has a disempowering effect on the family compared to conjoint treatment. This is another indication of conjoint treatment. As shown below, this situation sometimes happens with people that tend to be self-sufficient, cut off from the support of parents, friends or community groups, fulfilling the cultural ethos of self-contained individualism described in chapter 1. Even though each family member benefits from individual therapy, it may be detrimental to the family as a whole. A false impression of change may be briefly created. The higher the number of intervening therapists, the harder it is for the family to remain cohesive and in charge of its process. Each practioner has his or her own goals, making those external influences often uncoordinated. An old saying of Ackerman could be à propos here: Two analyses make for one divorce.

The Gilbert parents practically never saw each other, each busy in their separate professional work, which seemed to suit their marital situation. Even when they were together, they did not agree on anything except the problems of their only child, a seven-year-old boy who was depressed. This child was taken care of and overprotected by a nanny who was herself quite isolated, being alone in a foreign country with no legal papers. The boy's individuation was curtailed. He was not learning well in school and had no friends. The family was isolated. The parents had friends only at work and had no significant contacts with their family of origin, who lived far away.

Both parents and child were in psychodynamic psychotherapy, and it was as if the parents were communicating to each other through their own therapists who knew each other. Each therapist, responding to the particular needs of his patient and being a confidant could, in some way, be seen temporarily as a obstacle to communication between the family members. To a certain extent, the parents were prevented from dealing directly with their conflicts and finding their own solutions. This uncoordinated work seemed to increase the family fragmentation and the isolation of family members.

The family was contaminated by the same model of assistance that the family itself induced, losing the power of their reciprocal relationships. Would it not be more logical to try a family-focused intervention at the outset that could have led later to individual-based interventions, if necessary? Maybe a family approach would have helped create the therapeutic space necessary to enlarge the family space that was so constricted.

In systemic terms, one could add that a morbid atmosphere was emerging out of the family when the members were together that could not be grasped and dealt with when family members were seen individually (the notion of nonsummativity). In addition, the various therapists involved were not directly taking advantage of the family potential as a changing power.

☐ Families and Resistance in Psychotherapy

Symptoms can be seen as maintaining equilibrium in both the individual's intrapsychic and interpersonal system. Within this framework, a systemic understanding of the psychotherapy process adds to psychodynamic understanding and may shed a new light on the patient's resistance. In accordance with systems theory, it is expected that all family members, as part of an interdependant collectivity, are affected by what the patient is experiencing in individual psychotherapy, and a set of interpersonal feedback is triggered by which the family either accepts or resists the change (see below the case of Mrs. Lee, a depressed woman with a blaming husband). The multiple impact of behavior must be taken into account. As the ecologists say, "You can never do just one thing." One cannot change without changing their significant others. From an interpersonal-systemic perspective, resistance in individual psychotherapy may serve system-maintaining functions, such as keeping the patient into an idiosyncratic role in the family.

A mechanism of neurotic reciprocity or complementary illness in marriage may greatly interfere with change (see also chapter 3). A partner may resist change in case his or her emotional needs are dependent on the persistence of some pathological elements in the other partner. In studying the husbands of agoraphobic women, Buglass and colleagues (1977) found a small subgroup whose husbands showed abnormal jealousy and were impeding the treatment process.

These men became more jealous as their wives became less symptomatic and more autonomous. The authors suggests that these husbands reacted by becoming emotionally distant, which increased insecurity and created confusion in their wives. In such cases, the addition of marital therapy may be a better alternative than individual therapy alone. The reactions of each partner to the change of the other can be closely monitored and worked through, and a simultaneous adjustment made by both partners.

The interpersonal-systemic perspective as applied to the intergenerational transmission of problematic behavior may also help one to understand some treatment impasses. For example, loyalty and unresolved debts toward the family of origin may be carried forward into new relationships and may impede treatment (Boszormenyi-Nagy, Grunebaum, & Ulrich, 1991). The case of an adolescent with an unresolved need for vengeance from a previous generation, leading him to violence, is an example.

A change in the patient's complex interpersonal system is usually not required. If, however, the system contributes significantly to either the etiology, the aggravation, or the maintenance of the problem, the patient's significant others should be involved. A failure to do so may explain certain treatment deadlocks. When patients are in a position of dependence on their family, a family intervention may be needed to resolve strong family resistance.

☐ Depression and Conjoint Therapy

Depression can be used to illustrate the importance of the family in regard to understanding and treating mental illnesses, even though advances in the biology and psychopharmacology of depression have encouraged the clinician to discard its influence. The biological model, which currently prevails in psychiatry, can also make the involvement of the patient's relatives more difficult as it may be harder for them to see their contribution to some manifestation of the depressive illness or to its maintenance. Marital or family problems may be hidden and displaced on a family member's depression (Keitner & Miller, 1990).

The interface between biological models and the family is complex and needs to be discussed with nuance. There is a large amount of literature about the family burden created by depression. The presence of a parent with a major depression has a strong negative impact on the other family members (Downey & Coyne, 1990). Families are justified in complaining about illness, but they sometimes make things worse.

The success rate of individual treatments (drugs, psychotherapy, or both) of affective disorders is rather low: 36%–50% of improved patients relapse (Shea et al., 1992). Hypothesizing the neglect of interpersonal factors in the understanding and in the treatment of affective disorders, Prince and Jacobson (reported by Pinsof & Wynne, 1995) undertook a review of methodologically sound comparative studies of individual versus marital therapy for the treatment of women suffering of unipolar depression coupled with marital problems. The course of depression and the rate of relapse seem to be significantly related to family functioning (Keitner & Miller, 1990), especially to the marital relationship (Hooley & Teasdale, 1989). According to these studies, marital conflict is the single most important precipitating factor and one of the best indicators for relapse. When the partner is unsupportive, as in the case of the depressed woman described below, there are consistently more relapses, showing that the partner may have a significant influence on the likelihood of recurrence of depression.

Comparing the efficacy of marital therapy and individual cognitive therapy in the treatment of depression in maritally distressed and nondistressed couples, Jacobson and associates (1991) found a statistically significant decrease of depression in both groups. For nondistressed couples, however, cognitive therapy was more effective. In maritally distressed couples, both approaches were equally effective, while marital satisfaction improved at a greater rate in the distressed couples treated with marital therapy. These authors hypothesized that depression was alleviated in maritally distressed women by increasing marital satisfaction.

The phenomenology of couples in which there is a depressed partner has been well described. There is often an emotional distance between the two partners. The well partner tends to express marital dissatisfaction indirectly, as there may be a fear of hurting the depressed partner, or it may come out in an explosive way. There is often an imbalance of power, with the well partner supervising everything done by the patient. The depressed partner also tends to view oneself as unable to survive without the other partner, feeling totally dependent. Marital problems are then attributed to the illness, and the depressed partner thinks he or she is not entitled to have feelings, with fear of rejection if he or she does.

The involvement of the marital partner in the treatment of a depressed individual seems logical, taking into account the link between low recovery and marital dysfunction. Involving the marital partner may lead to a better appraisal of the situation and to a simultaneous change in both partners. The marital partner is often an essential resource in helping the depressed spouse. According to Lefebvre and Hunsley (1994), the partner has to regain confidence that the depressed spouse can get better, and that both can still do something to lift the depression. The power imbalance also has to be addressed and the depressed patient has to be reassured that feelings can be expressed safely.

Prince and Jacobson (1995) also tentatively concluded from their review of various studies, including Clarkin and colleagues (1990) randomized clinical trial, that severity of depression may predict response to conjoint therapy: Conjoint therapy seems more effective with the least depressed patients. They also reported that conjoint therapy is more cost effective than individual psychotherapy for depressed women in distressed marriages.

Mrs. Lee, an unemployed school teacher, was hospitalized for major depression after she made a suicidal attempt. Her husband lately had exploded at her repeatedly as he realized she was getting depressed again. She had been hospitalized many times before for depression and treated with medication and individual psychotherapy, which led to temporary improvement. Mrs. Lee was a poorly-adjusted woman and seemed to be in constant need of care. She saw herself as unable to survive without her husband, her dependency being reinforced by her psychiatric illness. She was the only child of a domineering and critical mother whose expectations she had been unable to fulfill. She had not known her father.

The family interview and the conjoint meeting with her husband showed the family influence in the maintenance and exacerbations of her depression. Even though her husband had good reason to perceive her as a burden, he treated her as a child and acknowledged her as much as she was submissive. Still he denied any marital dissatisfaction, his resentment being expressed through his relentless need to devalue her in front of their children.

In sessions, he interrupted her each time she spoke, disqualified her statements, and even ridiculed her, which seemed to contribute to her feelings of worthlessness and to maintain her depression. She was unable to be assertive and to set limits with her husband. Even though she was well-intentioned toward her two children, she had lost the significant and rewarding relationship she had with them when they were younger. The children remained closer to their father and did not respect their mother. They even refused to go out with her.

Involving Mr. Lee in the treatment, and to some extent her children, seemed a logical course of action and a sine qua non condition to her improvement. Mutual respect and Mrs. Lee's capacity for affirmation had to be reinstalled. At first, Mr. Lee refused to see a member of the treating team with his wife. He insisted seeing the doctor one-on-one and to transfer treatment responsibilities to the doctor. The psychiatrist met Mr. Lee and started at his level of understanding, which was that his wife was suffering of a biological disorder and he had nothing to do with it. The clinician kept insisting for conjoint meetings and after a few sessions, Mr. Lee finally agreed to see a social worker with his wife.

The couple selected a few specific areas to work on for a predetermined number (five) of sessions. Preventing blaming and self-blaming, the therapist established a structure and a therapeutic atmosphere in which each partner's perspective and their influence on each other's feelings were discussed. The family was also met, using a psychoeducational model. The social worker gave information about depression, which was specifically tailored to the family life experience and made the two children actively participate. With Mr. Lee present in the training sessions as an ancillary therapist reinforcing his wife's efforts to change, assertiveness training was also used. Mr. Lee became threatened as his wife showed some independence and wanted to get busy outside home. She had to reassure him that she was still going to take care of him and of the household, and that he would remain the provider.

The couple was using imbalance of power and the role of victim and victimizer to suit individual needs and some complementary interpersonal mechanisms described earlier. The depressive symptoms seemed to maintain a shaky marital equilibrium at the expense of Mrs. Lee's emotional equilibrium. The vignette also highlights the circular causality model and circular loops described in previous chapters. Mrs. Lee's depression was contributing to her husband's critical behavior, and the reverse was also true. The two clinicians involved in the case used a circular perspective to understand and treat Mrs. Lee. The treatment was integrative, combining drug therapy and support, marital therapy, and assertiveness training.

It is important to involve the offspring in the assessment, and, to a lesser degree, the treatment of depressed parents. The account given by depressed mothers of their family may be misleading. In individual interviews, they are usually not talkative and rarely express their resentment toward their children. As they tend to blame themselves and deny any negative influence of others in their problems, it may be hard to know the family environment without seeing their partner and the family (Keitner & Miller, 1990). Psychiatric consultations done in obstetrics to depressed mothers, for example, may have important shortcomings if these mothers are assessed without meeting their close relatives.

In their study of children of parents suffering from serious affective disorders, Downey and Coyne (1990) found that depression in one parent instills strong feelings in children, such as depression, despair, anger, and guilt. These authors found a surprisingly high rate of depression: As many as 50% of these children experienced an episode of depression by the end of their adolescence.

Family involvement may take various forms, such as a psychoeducation, conjoint therapy or participation in a self-help group. Beardlee and colleagues (1997) found that family interventions have a preventive effect on the children of families in which a parent had an affective disorder. In this study, families were randomly assigned to either a treatment in which a clinician met the whole family over 6–10 sessions and gave information specifically linked to the families' life experience, or to an intervention focusing on lectures given only to parents. In the first sample, children were actively involved in discussions regarding parental illness. Both treatments yielded a sustained effect 1.5 years later but the clinician-facilitated treatment was associated with more positive self-reported and assessor-rated changes than the lecture intervention. These findings show the importance of not only involving the patient's spouse but also the offspring, to at least make the family members aware of the normalcy of their strong feelings.

☐ Efficacy

The historical context of conjoint therapy did not promote clinical research, which could be why conjoint therapy has, until recently, failed to develop a strong research background. Most family therapy pioneers were opposed to the scientific method. Since conjoint therapy has gained some acceptance, there have been, however, a large number of studies validating its efficacy. Its overall effectiveness is now well established.

Conjoint therapy outcomes have been found to be as good as or better than other psychotherapeutic approaches for many types of problems. Many meta-analytic studies have shown considerable effect size (0.45 to 0.70) of marital and family therapy (MFT) (see, for example, Shadish, Ragsdale, Glaser, & Montgomery, 1995; Markus, Lange, & Pettigrew, 1990). Shadish and associates examined 163 controlled studies of marital (n = 62) and family therapy (n = 101) all involving random assignment and a clinically distressed population. Their data revealed an overall effect size of 0.51, which means that the odds of a client doing better in a family-based treatment than in no treatment at all are two out of three. An effect size this big is much larger than one usually finds in pharmaceutical outcome studies. The effect sizes for both marital and conjoint therapy were significant and not statistically different (Shadish et al., 1995). Furthermore, these authors did not find any scientific data to support the superiority of any one particular orientation to marital and conjoint therapy.

The effectiveness of conjoint therapy has been demonstrated in various psychopathological conditions including schizophrenia (see chapter 7), depression (see above), adolescent conduct disorders (see chapter 6), and drug abuse. Reviewing drug abuse outcome studies which included conjoint therapy treatment, Stanton and Shadish (1997) found, in their meta-analysis, that conjoint therapy was superior to individual therapy and peer group therapy. This treatment modality was effective with both adolescent and adult drug addicts, and was seen as a cost-effective adjunct to methadone maintenance.

In their review of 18 studies involving adolescent and adult drug abusers, some of which constituting controlled clinical trials, Liddle and Dakof (1995) found that the efficacy of family-based approaches was positive and significant. Four comparison studies of adolescent drug abusers showed the superiority of family-based interventions to peer-group and parent education at the end of the treatment and at follow-up. Liddle and Dakof (1995) found it impossible, however, to evaluate the specific impact of conjoint therapy, as the studies reviewed included other types of approaches such as individual and community interventions. For adult drug addiction, the efficacy of family-based approaches was not as evident as for adolescents. Liddle and Dakof argued that conjoint therapy appears more powerful with adolescent drug users because they have more contact with their families and usually have not been abusing as long as most adult abusers.

In a meta-analytic review of 21 outcome studies of family-involved therapy for alcoholism, Edwards and Steinglass (reported by Pinsof & Wynne, 1995) found not only evidence for the usefulness of this approach at all three phases of treatment (initiation, primary treatment, and aftercare), but also its cost effectiveness. Each study included a control group and objective outcome data about alcohol consumption after treatment. Reviewing empirical research on conjoint therapy with alcoholics, Alexander and colleagues (1994) also concluded that the addition of this therapeutic format suggests that couples receiving this treatment did better on both marital and drinking measures as compared to those who did not receive it. Edwards and Steinglass (1995) found that four comparative studies, specifically designed to evaluate family interventions to engage alcoholics in treatment, yielded convincing evidence in favor of involving family members and recommended such intervention be a routine part in the engagement phase of the treatment of alcoholics.

Although there is some evidence supporting the advantage of conjoint therapy over individual psychotherapy during the treatment for short-term abstinence, this superiority disappears after one year as any alternative treatment without aftercare (Pinsof & Wynne, 1995). In their meta-analytic review, Pinsof and Wynne finally found conjoint treatment superior to no treatment or to standard treatment aftercare for abstinence up to two years.

Conjoint therapy is also effective in emotional problems of different age groups from childhood to old age (for adolescence and old age, see chapter 6). From its origins conjoint therapy was closely related to the treatment of children because it was found that the power of the family can easily undo the benefits of the individual treatment of the child. Conjoint approaches are particularly useful when the children's problems are directly related to their parents' problem, or when they have a pathological role or excessive power in their family.

In their review of eight controlled outcome studies on childhood conduct disorder (CD) and in 13 studies of family interventions for attention deficit/hyperactivity disorder (ADHD), Estrada and Pinsof (1995) found uniformly positive results compared to individual treatment or to no treatment. In a meta-analytic study, Markus and associates (1990) also found conjoint therapy effective in a wide range of child problems. In their childhood CD review, Estrada and Pinsof found significant and positive changes in childrens' and parents' behavior. Surprisingly changes were retained in follow-up studies (up to 14 years in one study). For ADHD, they found that in most of the 13 studies they reviewed, conjoint therapy did not change the core symptoms of ADHD but rather noncompliance and aggression. Estrada and Pinsof also reviewed six studies comparing conjoint therapy to pharmacotherapy. In the short run, stimulant medication was found to be more effective and conjoint treatment did not increase the short-term efficacy of the medication.

Even though research shows the powerful influence of the family on physical health, family therapists usually have ignored physical illnesses and their linkage to the family. Reviewing the effectiveness of family intervention in the treatment of physical illness, Campbell and Patterson (reported by Pinsof & Wynne, 1995) reported that these interventions seem to be most effective in chronic chilhood illnesses such as asthma and diabetes. In two controlled studies of conjoint therapy in the treatment of children with severe asthma that approach was superior to standard care. As Campbell and Patterson (1995) reported, however, in most studies of pediatric illness, the attention-placebo effects were not controlled and the family approach was part of an integrative intervention from which the family treatment was not differentiated.

Family interventions were also found effective in the management of some cardiovascular and chronic neurological disorders in adults. Campbell and Patterson (1995) reviewed two controlled studies on hypertension and found the addition of the psychoeducational approach superior to standard treatment and to individual psychotherapy. In three large scale studies, family intervention was found better than individual dietary intervention to decrease cardiac risks factors (Campbell & Patterson, 1995). These authors added that empirical evidence clearly indicates that the psychoeducational intervention is the most effective approach in regard to family intervention for physical illness for both children and adults. They reported the results of four controlled studies involving children with asthma, diabetes, and other chronic illnesses and found the psychoeducational approach superior to standard treatment.

In an overview of empirical research on the efficacy of conjoint therapy, Pinsof and Wynne (1995) stated that this type of intervention is applicable to severe psychiatric conditions when combined with other treatments. They also concluded that conjoint therapy is more effective than standard and/or individual treatments for depressed outpatient women in dysfunctional marriages, marital distress (for that condition, conjoint therapy is also cost effective; Bray & Jouriles, 1995), alcoholism and drug abuse, adolescent conduct disorders, anorexia in young adolescent females (see chapter 6), and various chronic physical illnesses in adults and children. Pinsof and Wynne (1995) added, however, that these results "must be tempered by a variety of methodological problems with the research" (p. 610), such as small samples and sometimes lack of random assignment to experimental and control groups.

5

CHAPTER

Group Approaches

Human grouping is an important social phenomenon. As discussed in chapter 1, groups have always provided people with closeness and intimacy as well as support and relief from human suffering. Religious healers and medicine men always used group dynamics to implement their practice, while modern medicine, which replaced them, totally ignores these forces. Groups are a natural means to obtain mutual help. To face the ills of modern Western society, such as isolation and alienation, psychotherapists may have to modify their practice. Groups may be a better, more logical way to help individuals who are separated from their family of origin, and are in need of new interpersonal relations and a sense of belongingness.

Authors, such as Dies (1993), have mentioned pragmatic reasons to support the current importance of groups. To deal with the individual's increasing needs, which are often unmet by existing institutions or current therapeutic modalities, as well as the decreased availability of professionals, the group approach presents an interesting alternative. Group therapy is of increased importance in regards to managed care and other cost-containment programs (Dies, 1993). Dies argues that group therapy is more economical than individual psychotherapy and that for many emotional problems, it is equally effective. Comparing the utilization of staff time in individual and group therapy, MacKenzie (1995) concludes that group modalities save large amounts of practitioners' time. This may be due to the fact that a good part of the therapeutic work comes from the interpersonal work of the group members—their presence and their real-world experience. In group therapy, this is made possible by the presence of a trained professional who utilizes group process.

Various group modalities as they apply to the mental health field will be now described. Special attention will be given to self-help groups, which provide much-needed interpersonal support that individual psychotherapy cannot provide. The common curative factors found in various group modalities and their efficacy will be also presented. The nuts and bolts of group therapy, such as group selection and composition, stages of group development, techniques, and procedures will not, however, be discussed; the reader is referred to the *Handbook of Group Psychotherapy*, edited by Fuhriman and Burlingame (1994), for further details in that arena.

☐ Group Therapy

Group therapy is a microcosm of society in general. The relationships between group members are studied and changed, with the assumption that this change will generalize to relationships outside. All the major psychotherapeutic orientations have been applied to groups. In the psychodynamic model, the unconscious conflicts, the transference and the characterological defenses which appear readily in groups, are interpreted within a group setting. Psychodynamic group therapy is a valuable approach to integrate the understanding and method of psychoanalytic psychotherapy with the interpersonal components of the personality.

The most popular group approach is based on Yalom's (1995) interpersonal group model. The interpersonal model emphasizes group interaction and process, group members learning from each other, and the active and structuring participation of the therapist. Although the various orientations to group therapy appear quite different from each other, in practice they show a lot of similarities (see the Curative Factors section later in this chapter). In any case, group therapists are now using flexible and integrative approaches, mixing psychodynamic, humanistic–existential and interpersonal concepts, and techniques borrowed from a variety of sources (Leszcz, 1996).

Evolution

Group therapy was rediscovered during World War II as a practical way to treat military personnel at a time when there was a shortage of psychotherapists. Clinicians were, then, incited to do the same at the time of the first wave of discharging mental patients from the asylum post-War. During the same period, some psychoanalysts started to apply the psychoanalytic model to groups of patients. Experiential groups were an important social phenomenon in the 60s and the 70s in the United States. Their leaders were reacting against the formalism of psychoanalysis of that period and were under the influence of the counterculture movement and the upsurge of Eastern philosophies.

To paraphrase MacKenzie (1996), who has contributed to the scientific validation of the group therapy experience, group therapy's first wave of popularity was related to wartime necessity and the second wave to a social movement toward experiential events. The current third wave seems to be driven by scientific and economic factors. Still, according to Yalom (1995), "patients and many mental health professionals continue to underrate and fear group therapy" (p. 510).

Indications

To match the diversity of clinical problems, there is an enormous variety of group therapies, from intensive groups to crisis intervention groups. According to the American Psychiatric Association (APA) 1989 Task Force Report, group therapy can be used with schizophrenia, mood disorders, personality disorders, neurotic problems, addictions, and adjustment disorders. In fact, any Axis I and Axis II psychiatric problem can be treated by some form of group therapy, usually as an adjunct to other therapeutic modalities such as pharmacotherapy or as a specific phase of a therapeutic program. To Rutan and Stone (reported by Spitz, 1996), the question is not, "Should group be considered for this patient?" but, "Are there mitigating factors against considering group therapy for this patient?" (p. 84).

The Therapist's Role

The therapist's role is similar across the spectrum of group therapy. It is a central position. To Spitz (1996), who has reviewed managed care groups, the therapist has to accomplish a set of functions that allow the group work and preserve the group members' integrity. Whatever their orientation, which regulates their relative activity and transparency, group therapists take the interpersonal perspective into account. They facilitate affective involvement and group cohesion (Spitz, 1996). They also foster the attribution of meaning to the interpersonal experience of the group members through feedback and they create opportunities to change interpersonal behavior. Leszcz (1998) mentions other therapist's functions such as setting rules and norms, defining goals and the task at hand, taking charge when indicated, and taking into account the group developmental stages. According to Leszcz, self-disclosure and feedback must progress along the group developmental stages so as to prevent "instant intimacy or premature confrontation" (p. 205) before the group has reached some cohesiveness.

Groups for Chronic Psychiatric Patients

It is well known that schizophrenic patients who are treated on an outpatient basis often talk very little to the therapist, while they may talk more with other patients in the waiting room or in group therapy. By helping each other and seeing changes in other patients, people with schizophrenia fare well in groups composed of other schizophrenic patients (Stone, 1996); they do not do well in heterogeneous groups, however. In a group appropriate to them, they get support and continuity that is often lacking in a hospital setting.

In a recent book, Stone (1996) has emphasized the importance of group therapy for the chronically mentally ill in managed care. He argued that group treatment fulfills these patients' clinical needs and is cost effective. Stone described how an extended period of group therapy has a positive impact on these patients' interpersonal deficits, which may prevent decompensation and hospitalization. These groups provide a support system in and out of sessions, which individual interventions cannot provide. Very few clinicians, however, conduct group therapy with chronically mentally ill patients. This type of work is often seen as unchallenging, as it is not focused on insight. The more common types of groups for the chronic mentally ill patients (Stone, 1996) include: medication groups, social skills training groups, walk-in groups, time-limited groups, process groups, and psychoeducational groups.

☐ Experiential Groups

Experiential groups are based on the interpersonal model. They took a variety of forms such as T-groups in the 50s, encounter groups and Gestalt groups in the 60s and 70s, and new forms in the 80s. The movement flourished in California among young people aspiring to a community life and peace. Assuming that social ills were creating emotional problems for the individual, experiential groups were seen as

an oasis by group participants. Yalom (1995) commented that, by promoting intimacy in groups, their leaders were looking for ways to
fight individualism and the alienation of the Western cultures.

As described by Greenberg and associates (1994), experiential groups
aimed at improving interpersonal relationships and mutual trust, and
increasing acceptance and sensitivity to others. The influence and
value of these phenomenological experiences are shown in the fact
that their methods and techniques, such as the role of the therapist
as a facilitator of the group process and the use of nonverbal, action-
oriented, Gestalt techniques have been integrated into various psychotherapeutic modalities. This makes experiential groups worth
mentioning.

As described by Bugental and Sterling (1995), experiential groups
derive from the existential–humanistic movement and share the same
theoretical basis. This movement incorporates the philosophy of the
European existentialists and also includes the humanist movement focusing
on the unique characteristics of the individual as delineated by Rogers
(1951) in the early 1940s. To Rogers, it is important to make people
aware of their potential, and to promote their capacity for positive growth
(not necessarily healing and illness). The movement finally borrows
from the phenomenology movement, which attempts to address the
clients' ongoing awareness of their own experience as primary data
presumably without using theoretical formulations. The experience of
encounter and the here-and-now therapeutic dialogue among group
members, and between these members and the therapist, are central in
experiential groups (Yalom, 1995). Therapists try to be empathic and
warm.

Members and leaders of experiential groups, however, were usually
well-functioning professional middle-class people, in search of personal growth. They particularly wanted to improve their interpersonal
skills and increase their sensitivity. According to Stein and colleagues
(1982), experiential groups symbolize the cult of emotionality with
the assumption that exposure and free expression of feelings within a
group process can promote growth and human potential. Within an
anthropological perspective, the intense experience sought in these
groups resembles the intense emotional group experiences that were
part of the religious ceremonies in primitive societies. Group members
are also encouraged to *do* instead of only discussing, to take risks and
to behave differently (Greenberg et al., 1994).

The practice of experiential groups, however, may lead to excesses
such as total self-disclosure. As these groups are often led by people
with no professional background in therapy using powerful interpersonal processes and techniques without clinical nuances, they could

have negative effects on the participants (Yalom, 1995). To Lieberman (1994), their expansion in all directions and the poverty of their theoretical framework have not made them attractive to mental health disciplines and have contributed to discredit group therapy. The human potential movement still exists but it has lost its popularity. In the 1980s, large group awareness training, such as Lifespring, has flourished with increased commercialization to provide growth services.

☐ Self-Help Groups

Self-help groups are often defined as member governed, cost free, and made up of individuals who share the same problem or situation (Meissen & Warren, 1994). Essentially based on interpersonal relationships, self-help groups are a means of support in facing specific problems that would be much harder for the person to face alone. What creates the links in self-help groups, according to Katz (1993), is the belief that the group experience will allow the participants to work through their problems. Through the members, these groups provide not only a support but they also address the emotional needs that medication or psychotherapists cannot meet.

The self-help movement is a very popular interpersonal and social phenomenon that deserves a special place among the interpersonal approaches to treatment. The emergence of this phenomenon is worth exploring in regard to the current and future practice of psychotherapy and the changes in health delivery system. Contrasting self-help groups to traditional psychotherapies may also reveal the strengths and weaknesses of therapeutic methods. It should help professionals to better understand and deal with some patients' needs, which they may ignore in their daily activities and which self-help groups seem to address so well.

The present analysis of the self-help group movement has been inspired by Reissman and Carroll's (1995) book *Redefining Self-Help: Policy and Practice*, Powell's (1994) *Understanding the Self-Help Organization*, and Katz' (1993) *Self-Help in America: A Social Movement Perspective*.

Human services, especially individual psychotherapy, cannot respond to the huge demand for mental health care. Eleven million Americans suffer from depression, 10 million are addicted to alcohol, and 6 million are addicted to drugs (Reissman & Carroll, 1995). Self-help groups are a grass-roots interpersonal way to respond to the unrooted individual in search of the kind of support which used to be provided by the extended family, the general practioner, the church, and the neighborhood. According to Reissman and Carroll, the return to the tradition of community, spirituality, and religion (which is sometimes called the "new neighborhood") is a major theme that is related to the self-help movement.

Self-help groups are a major growing source of help for a variety of physical and emotional problems. The expansion of the self-help movement has been phenomenal. It is estimated that 7.5 million American adults have been involved in a self-help group at some time during their lifetime (Lieberman & Snowden, 1994). According to Lieberman and Snowden, substance abusers and people with affective disorders predominate among those who seek out this type of help. Based on the longitudinal Epidemiological Catchment Area (ECA) survey, Narrow and colleagues (1993) found that the use of self-help groups represented 12% of the total service use by people with a nonsubstance diagnosis and 20% among those with substance abuse disorders. Self-help groups have been predicted to become a major psychotherapy provider of the future and the motor of health prevention (Norcross et al., 1992).

Types of Self-Help Groups

Self-help groups are extremely varied. There are groups for abused people as well as for abusers of all kinds; for alcoholics, sexaholics, workaholics, gamblers, and overeaters. There are self-help groups for nearly all the major illnesses and for almost any health and social problem. Self-help groups are particularly useful for people coping with life crises and major transitions, such as separated spouses having to cope with custody battles or with raising kids alone, and older people. Groups focusing on after care and chronic conditions seem particularly important. This is an area where self-help groups have highlighted the inadequacy of traditional individual treatment based on the doctor–patient relationship.

Some groups deal with difficulties of living with an individual who has problems that include children's afflictions ranging from autistic disorder to cancer. The relatives can learn about the illness and share information and feelings with people who are in the same situation. Whatever the situation may be, these people often experience similar feelings, which can be alleviated by the group experience. The experience of other parents may also be useful for the caretaker in the management of the disabled individual.

In the mental health field, self-help organizations such as the National Alliance for the Mentally Ill (NAMI), play a important role. Self-help groups may be seen as a critique of many psychotherapies.

These groups reach mental conditions which are resistant to traditional psychotherapies, such as the addictions. Mental health self-help groups, however, can easily work in tandem with mental health services and can be seen as a significant adjunct to the professional treatment centered on individuals (Reissman & Carroll, 1995).

Alcoholics Anonymous (AA) is the prototype of the "anonymous" groups and has been adapted for various problems, other addictions in particular. To tackle some of the problematic features of the alcoholic person (denial of the problem, the loss of control over alcohol use), a very strict and concrete program is used. Gartner and Reissman (1977) have given a thorough description of the characteristics of AA groups: a high degree of authoritarianism, the blaming of the alcoholic who needs a behavior reform, a focus on symptoms, and the fact that individuals are held responsible for their behavior. Group cohesion and a positive group atmosphere are promoted to provide support. The program also provides directives to a way of living and to inculcate new values and personality changes that resemble a spiritual experience. The development of an alternate culture from which members can assert their identity is also fostered.

According to Lieberman and Snowden (1994), the classical picture of self-help groups such as AA, emphasizing egalitarianism and run by nonprofessional leaders sharing the common problem of the group is misleading and does not represent the current practice. Self-help groups are multifaceted and change over time. For example, there is an increased involvement of professionals in self-help groups. Based on the UCLA study, Lieberman and Snowden (1994) reported that 60% of self-help groups (not counting substance abuse groups) were led by professionally trained people.

☐ Curative Factors

In *The Theory and Practice of Group Psychotherapy*, Yalom (1995) proposes various factors that highlight the interpersonal perspective and are unique to groups to explain the therapeutic efficacy of group therapy. Some of these factors are:

1. *Universality.* Sharing their problems with others, individuals realize they are not alone and may feel relieved. This may be an important normalizing function. This consensual validation provides reassurance and may improve self-esteem.
2. *Interpersonal learning from group members.* Through comparison, group members can see how other group members think and feel.

Members may also accept feedback from other members who are are in the same position as they are more easily than from the group leader (see the case example of Ann below).

3. *Group cohesiveness.* The attachment that members form toward each other, the leader, and the group contributes to the group cohesiveness. This, in turn, creates an optimal interpersonal environment for meaningful relationships and for their acceptance of feedback.

4. *Altruism.* Group members come to realize that they make a contribution as they help each other through sharing and feedback.

Fuhriman and associates (1986) did a factor analytic study designed to reveal group members' perceptions of various curative factors. Their results revealed that Yalom's factors represent concepts that are relevant clinically and research-wise. These factors do not necessarily involve direct therapist–group member relationships. According to Dies (1994), it is the group that is the main agent of change and the therapist works more indirectly than in individual psychotherapy. An example illustrating the curative factors, in particular, the interpersonal learning and feedback from group members, at work in group therapy follows. The case also shows the strength of the interpersonal as a therapeutic lever described in chapter 3.

Ann, a 35-year-old single business woman, was referred by her therapist to a psychoanalytic group while receiving individual psychotherapy. Her therapist felt a group experience could hasten her recovery, as she had acquired some stability through individual psychodynamic psychotherapy. He also thought that group therapy could enhance her individual treatment because she could use individual therapy to discuss some disturbing feelings experienced in the group. She asked for psychological help, some years before, for feelings of isolation and multiple somatic complaints. As far as she could remember, she had always felt isolated. Unable to see her own contribution to her problems, she was constantly blaming others and showed contempt and envy toward them. She found her peers immature and inferior to her, but deep down inside, she felt the opposite.

Even though the group therapist managed to have affective involvement of group members and group cohesiveness, Ann remained aloof for a long time and missed a lot of sessions. She developed an erotic transference toward the group leader but felt despised by him as well as by the other group members. She was not ready to participate in the group work, which meant disclosing emotionally-charged experiences and sharing her vulnerability. To her, disclosing herself to a group was humiliating and would lead to being attacked and hurt. This was interpreted many times by the group therapist, but to no avail.

During one session that was particularly difficult for many group members, Ann inadvertently made a derogatory remark about all the group members. Remaining relational and respectful, and within the work ethic of that group, one member asked her if she realized the meaning and the impact of what she had just said. Ann was taken off guard at being confronted with her contempt for others. She excused herself and admitted tearfully how hard it was for her deal with feeling miserable and inferior to others. The group's empathic response to her display of vulnerability surprised her, and this intense emotional experience seemed influential to her subsequent attitudes toward the group and its members. Ann began to respond more respectfully to the other group members' emotional experiences. She started to attend the group regularly, and slowly ventured into expressing and sharing her problems.

The philosophy of the helper therapy principle (Reissman & Carroll, 1995) can be used to understand the mechanisms underlying some of the curative factors mentioned above, specially altruism. This philosophy is based on the notion that individuals in difficulties can help when they are offered the opportunity, such as when empowerment and lack of hierarchy are emphasized, and when their competence based on their life experience is valued (Reissman & Carroll, 1995). By seeing their own reflection in another member's struggling, individuals may also find the courage to delve into their own problems. In fact, the interchangeability of roles of the helper and the helpee, which allows each individual to experience each role, seems to be an important part of the efficacy in interpersonal therapy with groups of people.

According to Reissman and Carroll (1995), effective helpers develop a feeling of interpersonal competence as they become aware that they have a positive influence on others (this is probably what the group members felt when they realized that Ann's attitudes toward the group had changed over time). The dictum shared by many religions that it is better to give than to receive is possibly based on these mechanisms.

The transformation of needs into assets is another important factor of the helper therapy (Reissman & Carroll, 1995). In self-help groups, for example, the peer structure of these groups allows this to play a role, using the interpersonal experience of people who have overcome their difficulties to help others experiencing the same difficulties. Later, the helpee will become a helper for other people with the same problem. The specific peer structure created by members sharing a specific problem and life experience, and helping each other creates a strength in dealing with adversity.

☐ Efficacy

Group Therapy

Many meta-analytic reviews dealing with hundreds of psychotherapy outcome studies done in various settings have shown that group therapy is as effective as individual psychotherapy for the treatment of many emotional disorders (Fuhriman & Burlingame, 1994; Robinson, Berman, & Neimeyer, 1990; Piper, 1993). Reviewing seven meta-analyses produced in the last decade, comparing the relative effectiveness of group versus individual format, Fuhriman and Burlingame (1994) found no reliable differences between individual and group psychotherapy. However, two meta-analyses yielded contradictory conclusions, showing superiority for individual psychotherapy. Fuhriman and Burlingame argued that these two studies relied exclusively on cognitive–behavioral investigations and used group therapy as a convenient approach to apply predetermined treatment interventions, with no effort to incorporate unique characteristics known as therapeutic in the group format such as Yalom's (1995).

In a comprehensive review of controlled outcome research on the efficacy of psychotherapy for depression and the relative effectiveness of various forms of treatment, Robinson and associates (1990) found no outcome differences between group and individual psychotherapy. They analyzed studies comparing individual therapy to a wait-list control (16 studies, average effect size of 0.83), and studies comparing group therapy with a wait-list control (15 studies, average effect size of 0.84), indicating that the efficacy of group therapy was almost identical to individual psychotherapy.

In addition, Robinson and associates (1990) considered the effect of other important factors in research on psychotherapy, such as the researcher's allegiance, the diagnostic screening procedures, the therapist's training, the client's characteristics, and the attrition rates for treatment and control groups; they found no evidence that any of these factors systematically influenced the outcome.

Piper (1993) also reported that in methodologically-sound clinical trials, group therapy has been proven to be more effective than control conditions in treating a variety of emotional problems, with minimal differences among variations in treatment. Group therapy has been found to be effective with patients with chronic psychiatric illness, with depression (see above), with patients with characterological problems (see chapter 7), and a variety of other populations. Reviewing the empirical literature on group therapy, Dies (1993) concluded that all major orientations applied to group therapy are effective.

Still, some comparative studies reporting the efficacy of group psychotherapy are not exempt from methodological problems. It is not always clear whether the populations studied were comparable or reflected selected populations of patients related, for example, to patient's preference for a given approach. Random assignment to different therapies, which addresses this bias, was not always used.

Studying outpatient groups (supportive and pragmatic) for poorly-educated and unemployed patients suffering from chronic psychiatric problems and chronic physical health problems, and comparing overall medical utilization 12 months before starting group therapy and 18 months after its initiation, Weiner (1992) found an increase in overall use of psychotropic medication and a better attendance at the medical clinic (possibly related to the group therapist's efforts to coordinate service delivery). Yet, the increased use of outpatient psychiatric and nonpsychiatric services was easily offset by a dramatic decline in psychiatric and nonpsychiatric hospitalization, leading to a large overall cost saving. Weiner concluded that group programs for very disturbed psychiatric patients are economically sound.

In managed care terms, group therapy is a cost-effective and a therapeutically viable modality. Given the comparability of outcomes with individual therapy, MacKenzie (1996) suggested that group treatment should be the primary modality for time-limited psychotherapy.

Experiential Groups

According to Greenberg and colleagues (1994), who have reviewed the research on experiential psychotherapy, there has been little evaluative research of experiential groups and one cannot expect significant changes, unless done in small groups led by clinicians. In their review, these authors conclude, however, that experiential therapies are useful for a variety of disorders, specially depression and anxiety. They also reported some evidence that it is not the traditional nondirective, client-centered aspects of experiential therapies but rather the action-oriented, directive methods of the Gestalt approach that are effective. In reviewing the outcome studies of Lifespring, a large group resembling the encounter groups of the 60s and the 1970s, Lieberman (1994) found no evidence of its effectiveness in improving symptoms associated with mental illness.

Self-Help Groups

Overall, outcome research on self-help groups usually yields positive results (Goodman & Jacobs, 1994). Reissman and Carroll (1995) also reported improvement in various areas including general functioning, coping, and reduction of treatment service use such as hospitalization. Self-help groups are well accepted by consumers. Their popularity and personal testimonials imply that they use methods which suit lay people. Goodman and Jacobs (1994) commented that in terms of basic interpersonal processes, self-help groups are characterized by less skeptical and more empathic responses to each member's disclosures when compared with group therapies and individual therapies. There is a growing acknowledgment of the importance and the uniqueness of self-help groups by clinicians, even though mental health professionals seldom refer patients to self-help groups (Lee, 1995).

Self-help groups are not exempt from criticism. Some of these groups may undervalue the work of professionals, neglect the need for appropriate treatment, and turn away from scientific knowledge in favor of self-reliance and experiential knowledge. Rosenbaum, Lakin, and Roback (1992) have reported that in some of these groups, there is not enough control of what is going on, which may lead to forms of abuse. For example, a leader or a group member may exert a very negative influence on others.

What self-help groups do, though, is different from what clinicians do. They are not a "poor person's psychotherapy" or an "uninsured person's psychotherapy," according to Powell (1994, p. 15), who has made a review of research in this field. A combination of the two is often useful. They should be part of a comprehensive service delivery system. These groups cannot replace professional services but they provide alternatives where professionals are ineffective or too costly.

Self-help groups are economical, as the consumers are producers of what they consume (Powell, 1994). Members are empowered to give help and not only receive service. In this way, self-help groups may reduce the excessive use of professional services. Money wise, self-help groups are accessible when compared to the costly treatment made in institutions. To conclude, a quotation from Sidel and Sidel (reported by Gartner & Reissman, 1977) nicely summarizes the usefulness of the self-help movement:

> The self-help and mutual aid movement is a response to a number of different factors in our society which make human services unavailable or unresponsive to those who need them: the pervasiveness of technology and its rate of development; the complexity and size of institutions and communities, with their accompanying depersonalization and dehumanization; [. . .] and the professionalization of much which in the past was done by individuals for themselves and for one another. Self-help groups have made major contributions towards dealing with

problems which cannot be dealt with by other institutions in the society, and at the same time have provided people with opportunities for helping roles, roles which have become increasingly difficult to find in our society as more and more helping has been taken over by professionals (p. 1).

PART

III

APPLICATIONS OF THE INTERPERSONAL ORIENTATION

CHAPTER

Conjoint and Group Therapy Across the Life Span

The interpersonal approach to psychotherapy is particularly well suited to certain age groups. Because they are still dependant on their parents, conjoint therapy is obviously applicable to children and adolescents. To remain closer to the practice of most clinicians who do not see children in treatment, the interpersonal approach will be discussed here in its application to adolescents. Due to the elderly's need for care and support, old age is another period of life that responds well to an approach involving significant others or a peer group.

☐ Adolescence

Based on individualism as a central value, the classical psychoanalytic developmental theory of adolescence emphasizes the separation–individuation process (Blos, 1985). Adolescence is seen as a transition period involving a progressive loosening of the ties to the childhood love objects and the development of a stable identity and sense of self, leading to autonomy and attachment to people outside the family (Blos, 1985). As adolescents develop an identity of their own, a restructuring of their psychic functioning and a modification of the equilibrium between intimacy and independence takes place.

The classical theory that focuses on the individual task of adolescence may neglect the corresponding interpersonal family system task, that is, the reshuffling of family dynamics and roles to prevent lack of individuation or estrangement leading to isolation of the adolescent (Lerner et al., 1999). As the introjected parents are focused on, the "real" parents and the family relationships may be treated as constant across all individuals. The psychoanalytic developmental theory of adolescence may also minimize the importance of interdependence with others. The importance of parents and peers for the development of the adolescent is supported by empirical findings. Reviewing the scientific information about adolescent development, Lerner, Villarruel, and Castellino (1999) emphasize the needs of the adolescent for advice and validation of individuality and self, which are provided by adequate relationships with parents and by the peer group.

The peer group is an essential element of adolescence. Being in a transient state and easily influenced by their relational environment, the formation of groups is a major force for adolescents. This is confirmed by developmentally-based research (see La Greca & Prinstein, 1999). It is well suited for their developmental tasks, reaching psychological independence from their parents and developing attachments to their peers. Group membership is specially important for self-development and acquisition of social skills.

The importance of parents and peers as untapped resources in reaching and treating adolescents has been confirmed in a survey involving over 400 male and female adolescents in grades 8 and 11 (Villeneuve, Bérubé, Ouellet, & Delorme, 1996). Through a self-administered questionnaire, these "normal" adolescents rated parents and friends as major contributors to problem-solving and as the first source of information concerning emotional problems. Surprisingly, these findings were statistically significant for both younger and older adolescents. The importance attributed to the parents, in particular, seems to contradict the popular belief that assumes there are major psychological disruptions in family relations in adolescence.

Adolescence and Family Disturbances

The family system level of differentiation, which exists on a continuum from being undifferentiated to being optimally differentiated, plays a major role in the individual task of adolescence. The less differentiated the family, the more likely the adolescent will have difficulty separating–individuating. The family system's task is not easy, as the adolescent's world is more complex and changing, compared to the world of the younger child. Parents have to modify their role and change the rules to adapt to their adolescent's needs for more autonomy, such as decreasing their control and sharing responsibilities while remaining involved and setting limits (Lerner et al., 1999).

Within an interpersonal-systemic framework, many problems of the adolescent may be seen as both a failure of the adolescent to separate–individuate and a failure of the family system to adjust to this. As often seen in clinical work, the parents may be part of the problem because of their own difficulty separating from their adolescent. The vacuum created by the adolescent's move toward autonomy may be handled in various way by the parents. They may get closer to each other but, in the case of marital conflict, the separation can be harder for everyone involved, as the pathological organization of the family is threatened. If the adolescent is a buffer between battling parents, the empty nest period may become difficult for the parents.

The parents' inability to face their marital problems often creates important problems for adolescents (Boyum & Parke, 1999). The youngster may be triangulated in the marital conflict, with overinvolvement of one parent and negative attitudes of the other parent toward him. As a child, he or she may have been kept infantilized and immature in order to fill one of the parents' needs for intimacy. In adolescence, this parent may finally realize the inapproppriateness of the child's overdependence, wishing for a change, while the adolescent may be totally unprepared to do so. The adolescent may sometimes have to be freed from the responsibility of the parents' marriage and from being a surrogate spouse before any other treatment can be effective.

Some developmental crisis of adolescents may also indicate a family crisis, an interpersonal struggle between family members that may impede the developmental task of both the adolescent and his family. The adolescent's symptoms are often a plea for help for both the adolescent and the family and can be understood at both levels for a more effective treatment (see the case of Tim in chapter 4).

With other adolescent problems, such as antisocial or other serious behavioral problems, a disturbed family functioning is usually present (Patterson, Capaldi, & Bank, 1991). These families are often characterized by a problem of hierarchy of long duration with inadequate limit setting and deviance in one parent, factors mitigating in favor of involving the family in the treatment. Patterson, Capaldi, and Bank (1991) have shown how parents' attitudes may lead to antisocial behavior in the home, such as inadequate and coercive parental practices fostering aggressive child behavior.

In an elaborate and well-designed study to determine the relationship between differences in parenting styles and antisocial and depressive symptoms in adolescents, and comparing these experiences with genetic influences, Reiss and his team (1995) found that 60% of the variance in antisocial behavior and 37% of the variance in depressive symptoms could be accounted for by negative parental behavior directed toward the adolescent. The research design included 708 families with at least two same-sex adolescent siblings who were either monozygotic twins, dizygotic twins, ordinary siblings, full siblings in step-families, half siblings in step-families, or genetically-unrelated siblings in step families. The authors concluded that parenting behavior specifically directed toward each child in the family is a major correlate of symptomatic behavior in adolescents.

Individual versus Conjoint Therapy

Adolescence is a good time to involve the family in the treatment. There is empirical evidence on adolescent development supporting family interventions in disturbed parent–adolescent relationships. As summarized by Steinberg (1990), family relationships that maintain a secure and strong affective bond while tolerating the expression of the adolescent's individuality and disagreement facilitate healthy adolescent development.

The level of intervention, be it individual, family, or both, should vary depending upon the severity of the adolescents' psychopathology, their age, degree of differentiation from their family, and motivation. With severe conditions such as schizophrenia and affective disorders, individual treatment is more important but some family involvement is usually required. When the adolescent is motivated for help and has the strength to change self and family relations, the individual or group treatment is indicated (Beutler & Clarkin, 1990). This is more likely the situation with older adolescents.

To Beutler and Clarkin (1990), in regard to younger adolescents the more their family has to be involved; the less differentiation between the family and the adolescents, the more family involvement is needed as well. For example, with rigid parents unable to tolerate the adolescent's move toward autonomy, or with an overdependent adolescent, it may be more effective to work first at the interpersonal level with the involved family members than dealing with the adolescent on an individual basis.

Individual psychotherapy with adolescents is not easy. Even if this seems a logical way to help the adolescent, in practice, individual psychotherapy is often not feasible and is a frustrating experience for the therapist (Kazdin, 1994b). First of all, adolescents usually do not come to therapy on their own. This is somewhat inherent to their age group; they often do not ask for psychological help but are coerced by parents, school, or social agencies. To ask for help often means they have to admit their pain and permit the emergence of feared emotions such as anxiety or depression. The link between the task of individuation–separation and the necessity to get attached to the therapist is also problematic.

Open-ended psychodynamic psychotherapy of adolescents is difficult. Adolescents tend to drop out of treatment while those who stay are sometimes unable to establish a workable transference. The regression inherent to the analytic work is a threat to adolescents. To talk about their childhood, for example, may bring the fear of dependence and regression to the phase they just left. Cognitive–behavior therapy can be a good alternative and looks promising for depressed adolescents (Wilkes, Belsher, Rush, & Frank, 1994). It is important, however, to involve the adolescents' significant others in CBT so as to consolidate their changes.

Even when indicated, only a minority of adolescents get significantly engaged and complete individual psychotherapy. The attrition rate is high among youth (50–75% according to Kazdin, 1994b). Premature termination sometimes may be traced to a strict adherence to individual psychotherapy to the exclusion of other modalities. As a result, key issues that cannot be addressed within this modality are seen as untreatable. The problem of the adolescent being unsuitable for traditional psychotherapy or refusing help is often overlooked. Many clinicians wash their hands, arguing that there is nothing they can do, sometimes leaving families in difficult situations or simply referring them to the judicial system. Being totally controlled by the acting-out adolescent, some parents feel helpless and suffer undue anxiety.

Conjoint therapy may be an alternative for some of these resistant adolescents and the psychotherapist's limited maneuvering can then be improved. These adolescents may more readily accept to come with their families and, in the case of refusal, their relatives may force them to come. The parents may even come alone for a while if necessary. Using family engagement strategies prior to starting conjoint therapy with Latino adolescent drug addicts in treatment, Szapocznik and colleagues (1988) increased attendance at the first session by 40% over a control group. They also identified four different types of resistant families and developed strategies for each type, resulting in better therapeutic outcome.

Structural work with the family, such as realignment of roles and the detriangulation of the adolescent, could strengthen the parents' alliance. This, in turn, can decrease the adolescents' omnipotence. Individual treatment of disturbed youngsters may become more feasible later on, as their problems are disentangled from the family's problems, and as they finally acknowledge their difficulties. The removal of some externalized symptoms may prepare them to reach more internal conflicts and to form a therapeutic alliance. As with children, the involvement of the family in the treatment of adolescents, especially young adolescents, is geared to promote their growth and the competency of the family.

Conjoint Therapy and Depressed Adolescents

Conjoint therapy is a useful treatment for depressive conditions of adolescents, as the effectiveness of pharmacotherapy is still not fully proven. Even though selective serotonin reuptake inhibitors (SSRI) antidepressants have been shown to be effective in the treatment of major depression in adolescents, so far, only a few double-blind, randomized, placebo-controlled studies have proven their efficacy (Emslie et al., 1997). In Emslie's and colleagues study, many patients had only partial improvement and only 31% reached full remission. Moreover, the wide standard deviation of endpoint means suggests that a multimodal approach is more appropriate.

A period of observation is often suggested before starting an adolescent on antidepressant medication, to ensure that the depression is major and is not mainly related to family or to other stressors. A family assessment may help appraise the various dynamics involved more quickly than relying only on individual assessment of the adolescent and on the parents' report of their adolescent's behavior (see the case of Corey below).

In addition to individual psychotherapy, certain depressed adolescents may benefit from a concurrent family approach that emphasizes growth and flexibility. When individual psychotherapy fails and the family appears to be contributing to the adolescent's depression, conjoint therapy may also be a good alternative. The treatment of depressed adolescents without the significant involvement of their close relatives is still, however, a common practice.

> Jason, 13, had many odds against him. Even though placed in a school for learning-disabled children, Jason was doing poorly compared to his schoolmates, had no friends and was always in trouble with his peers. The boy had a very poor self image. He blamed himself but he could not stop his repetitive behavior. He also felt rejected at home. His mother could not tolerate her son's behavior any more. Jason was demanding, never satisfied with what he got, and was stealing money from her. The mother had many other stresses, including a serious back problem that impeded her functioning at work and at home. Jason was blamed for everything wrong in the family and negatively compared to his idealized

eight-year-old sister. Overwhelmed and not knowing what to do, the father occasionally beat his son once a while. Jason's teachers became worried when the boy started to withdraw and to talk about suicide.

Jason was referred for psychological help and was assessed both alone and with his mother. Antidepressant medication was not indicated, but Jason was seen as a good candidate for individual psychotherapy, as it seemed that the empathy and understanding that he badly needed was not provided at home. Jason's mother was also referred for counselling. The treatment started but failed after a few weeks. Jason did not want help any more and his mother found various excuses for missing her apointments.

A family assessment was done and Jason's father, out of despair, volunteered to come to therapy with his son. He was seen with Jason in conjoint therapy with a male therapist. At first reluctant to miss work to attend therapy, the angry father slowly became attuned to his son's feelings and became deeply involved (see chapter 8 for details on how the therapist managed to engage the father). The father became more interested in Jason's athletic abilities, especially soccer, which helped minimize the focus on the boy's poor school performance.

Due to the father's limited time availability and Jason's poor motivation, a short-term, problem-focused approach was used. Problems were identified in behaviorally-specific terms relevant for their resolution. For example, the father managed to get a brief note of Jason's attitudes in school and reinforcers promoting father–son rapprochement were used as incentives.

This approach may appear simplistic in dealing with an adolescent presenting problems that do not readily lend themselves to quick solutions. However, with budget cuts, clinicians have to deal with this type of complicated problems within a very restricted period of time. They have to use approaches that easily lend themselves to brief interventions, such as conjoint therapy. Both the father and the son became active participants in this process, which enhanced their sense of personal efficacy and active mastery. This speeded up the therapeutic process. Like many adolescents of his type, Jason was not a good candidate for explorative psychotherapy and he was not even interested in coming to therapy alone. A short-term conjoint approach fostering relationship and based on behavior and action was indicated.

The father–son relationship became a strong therapeutic lever. Mobilizing father–son resources eventually helped stabilize Jason. They were seen once a week over a period of two months and then once a month. Other therapeutic alternatives were available. However, to help the father in his role of parent was more natural, and probably more beneficial, in the long run.

Conjoint therapy and adolescents in crisis. A family-based approach is also very useful in crisis intervention, especially with adolescents. A suicidal attempt or other dramatic acting-out behaviors, usually a cry for help for both the patients and their families, often precipitates or intensifies a family crisis. When seeing these patients in emergency situations, the clinician must go beyond the linear medicolegal dimension. Besides the nosographic classification and the need to evaluate suicidal or homicidal risks, to admit the patients or to send them home, the symptoms must also be explored in the context of a metaphor for a crisis involving the patients' immediate relational environment. Out of context, a symptom may otherwise be wrongly perceived as a major sign of a psychiatric illness.

Corey, 17, the only son and the second child of immigrant parents, took various medications used by his mother and went to bed with the idea of dying. As Corey's mother heard him vomiting, she went into his room and he was rushed to the hospital. Considered suicidal and possibly suffering from a major depression, Corey was admitted to the psychiatric ward for observation. He had been missing school lately with somatic complaints, an inability to concentrate, and to keep up with the demands of his school. Corey also linked his suicide attempt to his recent break up with his girlfriend, and his feeling of loneliness since his sister left home two months before. He was very vague about his family.

On the day following Corey's admission, his family was met as part of the routine work up of the Crisis Intervention Team. The extreme tension between the family members was denied by everyone except Corey's sister. The father declared that there had never been any friction between him and his wife, even though they both seemed frustrated and distant from each other. They obviously had displaced their frustration on their son and formed a strong coalition against him, blaming him, and not showing any empathy toward him.

The father was domineering and negative toward Corey, and the mother agreed. Both parents, especially the father, were disappointed with their son's academic performance, even though he had always been an A student. There was a cultural element in the parents' high expectations for their son, from which Corey's sister was spared. While giving a great deal of emotional power to his parents, Corey was unable to express his long-repressed resentment against them, as any protest was curtailed by the rigid family system. As his sister was now outside the family, she was able to speak out for him. She felt Corey was a prisoner of the system and she thought he came to see suicide as his only solution.

During Corey's three-day hospitalization, the family was met every day. During these family meetings, Corey finally expressed some negative feelings, which paved the way for his mother to express her own pain. It became obvious that Corey's suicidal gesture was also expressing a crisis involving the whole family. The sister's abrupt departure from home, in itself symptomatic of the disturbed family functioning, had left the mother feeling increasingly isolated. The daughter had always been supportive of her mother, but lately felt she couldn't handle it any more. The crisis intervention momentarily freed Corey from his idiosyncratic role of being a scapegoat, liberated some of his potential for growth, and brought some alternatives to the family. The intervention had a structuring and reassuring effect, which allowed Corey's quick discharge from the hospital with provisions made to continue tackling his intrapsychic and family problems.

Interviewing and actively involving the family in the crisis intervention often bring new meaning to the symptom, and unexpected developments. The interpersonal-systemic perspective used here often helps go beyond the linear model and the determinism of psychiatric nosologies. Crises are multifaceted. They imply risk, regression, and chaos, but they also bring the possibility for openings, progression, and reorganization. This phenomenology is well illustrated in Corey's case. A breach momentarily may be opened in some families, not usually sensitive to their adolescent's suffering. This leaves the family members more vulnerable, but at the same time, more open to change. A short-term family intervention may, then, become possible.

Sibling subsystem therapy is another interesting application of the interpersonal approach in adolescents, using dynamic elements of both conjoint therapy and of the peer group. This modality may be useful when the index adolescent is not a candidate for individual psychotherapy and will not cooperate in conjoint therapy. Adolescents who are silent or oppositional in therapy may respond more positively when seen with their siblings.

Finally, adolescence is a stage when the integration of various forms of psychotherapy is useful, and sometimes necessary. Individual psychotherapy may allow the adolescent to deal with intimate matters, while conjoint therapy may help them distancing from the family. Group therapy, used alone or along with another approach, can also be part of this integration.

Group Therapy

Peer-oriented group therapy for adolescents is surprisingly little used in clinical setting. The adolescents' sense of self is almost inseparable from peer relationships, which gives weight to an interpersonal approach to therapy, especially group therapy (Kazdin, 1994b). That therapeutic modality has specific advantages over other forms of psychotherapy with adolescents. Group therapy may tap the adolescents' need for acceptance and sharing, because adolescents easily become mutual psychotherapists for one another. Feedback from other group members is more easily accepted and usually carries more weight than feedback from parents or professionals. As compared to individual psychotherapy, this feedback is usually more concrete and varied.

Among the curative factors delineated by Yalom (1995), interactions with others and self-disclosure in the group have been reported as very important by adolescents (Corder, Whiteside, & Haizlip, 1981). Sharing emotions and ideas helps to develop mutual trust and reciprocity, and can be very supportive for the emotionally-disturbed adolescent. For example, adolescents who think they are the only ones who have problems, or adolescents who feel rejected may benefit greatly from group participation.

> Tony was an isolated older adolescent living alone with his depressed mother. He had poor social skills and felt easily victimized. Following assessment, he was referred to an adolescent group, which included six other male and female adolescents who were presenting either acting-out or neurotic symptoms. The group leader, a woman, was using an integrative approach based on a psychodynamic and interpersonal orientation. Tony felt shy in the group and was obviously intimidated by the presence of female members. Outside the classroom, he had minimal contact with girls. As one of the female members was presenting a symptomatology similar to his, he was able to have some interactions with her. They were quickly singled out as different by some other group members who became sarcastic toward them. With the therapist's support, they managed, however, to fend for themselves, which helped Tony develop some confidence in himself.
>
> Tony's central relational problem, however, remained untouched as he felt again a victim and rejected by the other group members. He was not aware, however, of his own contribution to the other members' reactions toward him. His oversubmissive stance and peculiar laughing whenever a feeling was expressed in the group were irritating to some group members. This was spelled out many times by one adolescent and modulated by the group leader. When the group learned about Tony's background and his miserable family situation, negative remarks addressed to him stopped and some members showed some empathy and willingness to help him. When the six-month duration group therapy ended, Tony was more integrated into the group.

That group experience was useful to Tony. He came to therapy feeling isolated, different from others, and with a low self-esteem. Sharing with a female group member the same problems and somewhat similar family backgrounds made him feel less different and less isolated. He got some sense of being part of and accepted by peers, which suited his developmental task of distancing from his depressed family environment and acquiring some social skills. No other psychotherapeutic modality could have provided him with such an experience. Some curative factors common to therapy groups (see chapter 5) were at work here: the therapist had managed to build a cohesive group, which allowed an optimal environment for self-disclosure, interpersonal input from other group members, and affective sharing.

Most adolescents can be considered candidates for group psychotherapy unless otherwise indicated (Kymissis, 1993). For example, group therapy is a logical and viable approach to many chronic conditions, physical or mental, that may plague the adolescent. To Kymissis, it seems easier, though, to define exclusion rather than inclusion criteria. The psychotic adolescent cannot be a candidate for that therapeutic modality.

Efficacy of Conjoint and Group Therapy

According to Diamond and his associates (1996) who reviewed family-based outcome research on the subject, the family approach is effective and increasingly applicable to a variety of problems in adolescents, such as drug abuse, eating disorders, depression, and conduct problems. By 1996, three meta-analytic studies showed that, on average, families treated with family-based treatments improved more than 67% of families treated with alternative treatments or no treatment at all (Diamond et al., 1996).

As reported by Pinsof and Wynne (1995), conjoint therapy seems to decrease adolescent conduct problems as compared to traditional treatment. These authors based their conclusion on previously published meta-analytic studies, in particular, Chamberlain and Rosicki's (1995). Chamberlain and Rosicki reviewed seven studies involving control or comparison groups, a manualized method of family therapy, and multiple outcome measures. These authors were cautious, however, in the interpretation of the results due to the methodological problems of the studies reviewed, such as small sample sizes and, in one study, matched comparison versus random assigment. Pinsof and Wynne also reported that family involvement (or at least some forms of it) is cost effective, compared to standard treatments and is most likely to help adolescents with moderately severe conduct disorders. Used alone, conjoint therapy is least likely to help the most severe cases.

Many studies have demonstrated the superiority of family-based treatment over standard treatments for reducing drug use (see chapter 4). Family treatment has a lower attrition rate than peer group treatment for drug abusers (between 11% and 30% versus 49% to 56%; Diamond et al., 1996). In regard to anorexia nervosa, Campbell and Patterson (1995) reported the results of three randomized outcome studies, previously done with adolescents, that show statistically significant results with the use of conjoint therapy. In one of these clinical trials, Russell and his associates (1987) compared family treatment and individual psychotherapy of anorectic and bulimic patients, and found the family treatment more effective posthospitalization for adolescent patients, and individual treatment better for adult patients. In both groups, an equal number of patients were still living with their parents. For bulimia, Pinsof and Wynne (1995) reported that neither conjoint therapy nor individual psychotherapy appears to be effective.

Only a few empirical studies have dealt with the efficacy of group therapy with adolescents. Most reports are anecdotal and observational. In a meta-analysis of nine studies with a total of 349 young subjects that compared group, individual, and control treatments in pre- and posttest design, Tillitski (1990) found both group and individual therapy effect sizes twice as large as those for controls. Although there was little difference between the two modalities, group therapy seemed more effective with adolescents and individual treatment more effective with children.

☐ Old Age

A negative attitude toward older people, sometimes termed "gerontophobia," is prevalent in psychotherapy (Garfield, 1994). Society is youth- and performance-oriented, which may lead to the neglect of older people. Clinicians are not inclined to treat seniors, and, for various reasons, may think they have nothing to offer. Lazarus and Sadavoy (1996) have commented that older people are often considered by primary care physicians as lacking the necessary resources to undertake psychotherapy. According to Sadavoy (1994), single interventions alone are usually inadequate with seniors with emotional problems and the frail elderly who cannot function independently, which shows the importance of involving the elderly person's significant others.

There are more older people in the United States now than ever, and the older population is growing at an accelerated rate (Longino & Mittelmark, 1996). Based on a 1991 U.S. government document, Longino and Mittelmark reported that it is anticipated that by the year 2030, there will be as many persons over 65 as there will be under 18.

For many reasons, old age is another period of life that seems suitable to an interpersonal approach to psychotherapy, be it conjoint or group treatment. First of all, referrals are usually made by family members and not by the elderly themselves, who may not think that they need help. Moreover, aging is not only an individual matter or a unigenerational problem; it concerns all the family members. The role played by the family in influencing illness is often underestimated, especially when organic brain disease is present (Asen, 1997). The clinician must adopt a larger perspective and also take into consideration the impact of the aging patient on each generation. For example, the family as a whole, and each of its members, is affected by the burden of care for the elderly.

Interpersonal Needs of the Elderly

Older people are in need of care and support, and this is of major importance to their well being. They need the presence of a person who is attuned to their demands, somebody to talk to who listens to them and is a confidant. This person accompanies them and helps them cope with their fears and mourn their losses. Western society, however, is not geared to support grieving, especially that of the loss of a spouse. Elderly people may try to do it on their own, as in an individualistic society people have been trained to be self-sufficient early on. This becomes impossible because of their relative limitations. They may adhere rigidly to previous roles and to deny any limitations, which may be accompanied by various negative feelings (Butler & Lewis, 1991). The problem may be compounded by the fact that the elderly often feel they are a burden to their family, as modern society has taken away some of their traditional roles of guidance and wisdom (Hargrave & Anderson, 1992).

Another extreme position may also be taken. The elderly may become totally dependent and helpless, conveying to the caretaker the older person's inability to cope, and intensifying the caretaking behavior. This increases the power of the elderly and places the caretaker in a difficult position. In any case, a role reversal is often present between the adult children and their aging parents who become dependent on their children. This role reversal sometimes leads to the infantilization of the elderly. Both positions—the pseudoindependence and the overdependence of the elderly—may cause great stress for the caregivers (Goldstein, 1996).

As reported by Golstein (1996), research shows that the majority of frail older people are cared for in the community by family members who may have to devote their life to the care of the sick member. These family caregivers, most frequently a wife or a daughter, have been identified as "hidden victims," submitted to stress created by the needs of patients in declining health. Confused older people, in particular, may heavily strain those who care for them. Family members may find it easier to tolerate a bedridden senior than an active, mentally confused elderly individual demonstrating disturbing behaviour (Deimling & Bass, 1986). Care of a patient with Alzheimer's disease, for example, may last two decades and is very demanding on the caregiver. Research has shown that caregivers have more psychiatric and health problems than members of a control group (Anthony, Zarit, & Gatz, 1988).

The caregivers of mentally-ill senior citizens are irreplaceable, but services to help them are underprovided under managed care or other cost-containment programs (Golstein, 1996). Even though educating and supporting caretakers is of prime importance, textbooks and review articles hardly discuss this topic. The emphasis is on the individual treatment of the elderly. So, clinical work with older people means working with the caregivers as well, sometimes seeing them conjointly. This type of work does not usually attract clinicians who are not prepared for it and do not see it as part of their mandate.

Conjoint Therapy

Sixty percent of referrals to geriatric services are related to psychosocial problems such as retirement, bereavement, or family conflict (Ratna & Davis, 1984). It seems more logical to tackle these referrals as both an individual and a relational problem, and to focus on the elderly, the family, and the social network. Therefore, the assessment should include the elderly's relational environment (Goldstein, 1996). In addition, crises which are so frequent in old age may hide family problems. A quick symptomatic relief may, then, obscure these family problems which are better dealt with interpersonally. Until recently, however, family members were often used only to gather information.

Anderson and Hargrave (1990) described how within an interpersonal framework the treatment is akin to what is done with children. The older person is seen as in need of the other family members and the clinician will use the family resources, compared to a perspective that sees the older patient as being separate from the family. The clinician may foster and harness family resources, for example, promoting more male involvement in the care of the elderly. Family legacy that influences who should be the primary caregiver often allows men to escape this involvement (Asen, 1997).

The aim of psychotherapy with older people is usually to offer a place where they will be listened to, supported, and helped to cope with reality without trying to change mental functioning. This can often be achieved with the help of significant others or through a group of seniors. Helping seniors' caregivers may take the form of counselling, especially psychoeducation done in groups.

The psychoeducational approach leads to the understanding of the psychological changes of the elderly, such as emotional lability and, in the case of Alzheimer's disease or dementia, disinhibition and concrete thinking. The approach also educates families about the stresses usually experienced by the caregivers and gives information about ways to cope (Leszcz, 1996). When conducted in groups, a psychoeducational approach can be highly supportive for the caregiver who has to deal with strong emotions raised by living with these patients (Perkins & Poynton, 1990). An exchange of ideas and suggestions about management is then facilitated. Family caregivers need to share their experience and be recognized for what they do for their relatives.

There is sometimes a recursive loop between the problems of the elderly and family functioning, each one negatively influencing the other. In these situations, family consultations reveal this circular reaction and enable the family to take better-informed actions (see the case of Mrs. Clark, below). Some families with significant intergenerational problems in the past may need reconciliation. If conjoint therapy is used, it may be important to review the life history of the elderly and to acknowledge the perspective of each involved family member in order to facilitate healing. Each generation can be validated in their past experience, and this experience can be made acceptable to all family members. Family sessions usually decrease anxiety and prevent the negative spirals that can easily develop.

Personality disorders represent a significant proportion of the psychiatric problems encountered in the geriatric population. There is a minimum of between 10% and 20% of personality disorders as a comorbid condition among psychiatric elderly patients (Fogel & Sadavoy, 1996). In these cases, conjoint therapy becomes even more helpful (see chapter 7). Character pathology is often exacerbated in old age as an increased need for care is experienced. The relatives may find it very difficult to deal with an elderly family member who is overly demanding or manipulative. Somatic and hypocondriacal concerns, for example, may become a powerful tool in order to get attention and extra care. In these situations, involving the family in the treatment is necessary in order to contain the patient's pathological behavior through a cohesive family and clinician's approach.

Mrs. Clark, a 68-year-old, was brought to psychiatric emergency many times over the past six months by her son, Robert. She was undergoing psychiatric treatment for feeling depressed and vaguely suicidal, and had many psychosomatic and hypocondriacal symptoms. She lived alone in her own home but Robert, his wife, and their two teenagers were living on the second floor. Due to his own anxiety, Robert had completely submitted to his mother's increasing demands since her husband's death 10 years before, and even more so since she was diagnosed with breast cancer for which she had been successfully treated.

In spite of his wife's criticims and his children's increased aloofness, Robert was available to his mother 24 hours a day and frequently had to leave his job to rescue her. Robert's wife had given up trying to change him, but his constant preoccupation with his mother had brought about a good deal of marital tension. He was stuck in a negative recursive loop with his mother. The more he did for her, the more helpless she felt and the more she blamed her son, which led to more marital and family tension. Robert became overwhelmed by the situation even though he was meeting his mother's doctor regularly and in despair, accompanied his mother to the psychiatric emergency room to relieve his anxiety.

The family evaluation revealed how Mrs. Clark's problematic behavior was maintained and the various systemic levels involved. For example, Robert's overinvolvement with his mother was found to be a way to fill the void created by his children's distancing themselves from the family. The treatment plan was changed. Mrs. Clark was met weekly with her son's whole family.

A few family sessions were more effective than individual counseling in changing some of son's attitudes and bringing more family cohesiveness in dealing with his mother. The sessions focused on the recursive loop between Mrs. Clark's problematic behavior and the family functioning. His wife's reluctance to be more involved with Mrs. Clark and share the burden with her husband was also discussed in therapy. With the therapist's support, better limits were set to Mrs. Clark's demands and concrete measures were taken to share the load of supervising her. Through some education provided by the therapist during family sessions about older people's depression and anxiety, the family became better aware of ways to cope with Mrs. Clark's problems. Robert was able to challenge his mother to do certain things by herself.

This vignette shows that family involvement with elderly individuals presenting some personality problems must emphasize a firm therapeutic structure, flexibility, and family cohesiveness. This is described in more detail in the following chapter, which deals with personality disorders.

Group Therapy

Group therapy for the elderly is a valuable modality that is used in many settings such as social agencies as well as residential and community centers. According to Leszcz (1996), who has written extensively on the subject, social isolation, interpersonal alienation, and the absence of a confiding relationship associated with depression in the elderly, may be particularly well addressed in group therapy. There are many types of group therapy for the elderly, from psychodynamic to cognitive, and including reminiscence group therapy and groups for burdened caregivers. In reminiscence group therapy, elderly people have the opportunity to review and reframe their lives. Reconnecting their past to the present may help with their loss of self-worth and their feeling of purposelessness.

Many group experiences, especially when done with one's peers, are better adapted to the elderly than individual approaches (Leszcz, 1996). They can provide the elderly with the support and empathic acknowledgment of their problems that they need. Group therapy also provides the opportunity for relatedness, which is often lacking in older people. Older people can share this stage of their lives together, have the opportunity for socializing, and decrease their feelings of loneliness.

Leszcz (1996) has also described how group experiences are particularly well suited for those with recent losses or individuals struggling with issues of retirement or a change in social network. Even though bereavement in post-parental people may be done either individually, in a family, or in a group setting, the presence of more than one person may facilitate listening, support, and finding new meaning in life. For the elderly, it seems natural and logical to cope with the loss and isolation that plague this age group through sharing common experiences with their peers.

Efficacy of Conjoint and Group Therapy

Reviewing family intervention outcome studies for demented elderly people, Campbell and Patterson (1995) did not find any controlled study of traditional family therapy for this population. They found, however, seven controlled studies of family psychoeducational interventions that primarily involved group sessions. These programs significantly reduced emotional distress and depression in caregivers, and increased problem-solving ability and feelings of mastery.

In meta-analytic studies of therapeutic interventions with depressed elders, group work produced a significant effect size of 0.78 in comparison to placebo or to no treatment (Scogin & McElreath, 1994). Reviewing outcome research studies, Leszcz (1996) concluded that the effectiveness of group therapy is shown through greater personal engagement, a decrease in self-absorption, and an improved capacity to verbalize affects.

Like conjoint therapy, group intervention is becoming part of time-effective and cost-effective ways to care for the elderly. These interpersonal modalities should help decrease the elderly's monthly or bimonthly visit to their medical doctors "for needless checkups and tests to allay their anxieties, overcome isolation, and find support from someone who is concerned with their welfare" (Gurfein & Stutman, 1993, p. 594).

Conjoint and Group Therapy and Some Psychiatric Conditions

Self-contained individualism cannot provide a cure for the enormous problems that the mentally ill and their families face in our culture. Some psychiatric conditions, such as personality disorders and psychosis, necessitate a multimodal approach, and the involvement of these patients' relatives is often a necessity. The suitability of an interpersonal approach involving significant others in the treatment of personality disordered patients will be reviewed first and the interpersonal treatment of these patients as it applies to families and groups will then be discussed. The second part of this chapter will focus on other chronic mental illness. The rationale for involving these patients' families, the impact of chronic mental illness on families, how these families are still blamed or ignored, and ways to involve them in the treatment also will be discussed.

☐ Personality Disorders

Working with families of personality disordered patients, I obtained experience, sometimes unwillingly. My colleagues were referring to me their worse cases and at the time I was trying to develop conjoint therapy in a setting where this therapeutic modality was somewhat unwelcome. Until then, I had not been convinced that active involvement of these patients' relatives in the treatment could be of any help. During the course of some of these difficult and often lengthy therapies, unexpected alternatives sometimes came out to change the gloomy atmosphere that often prevails in the families of patients with personality disorders. Their singularities being used, some of these families were freed from predicted constraints, which activated their potential for growth and their creativity.

These patients form a small portion of the psychiatric clientele but they mobilize a disproportionally high amount of available resources (Segal & Weideman, 1995). Borderline patients, in particular, are very difficult to treat because of their discriminating characteristics such as abandonment/engulfment concerns, entitlement, and regression in treatment (Gunderson, 1984). Because the inappropriateness of emotional response and interpersonal dysfunctioning do not necessarily produce distress in patients with personality disorders, there is a great variation in their motivation for treatment. As they usually perceive the difficulties as outside in others, these patients do not see themselves as having problems but still may seek consultation because they feel depressed, misunderstood, or anxious.

Being unable to tolerate the patient's complaints or accusations, feeling confused and not knowing how to avoid the patient's negative reactions, other family members such as a spouse or a parent, or sometimes a co-worker, may suggest a consultation for reasons often different than those expressed by the patient. When they face loss, people with personality disorders, especially borderline personality disorder, are unable to self-soothe. The actual presence of a significant other is necessary. They use projective defenses to explain their behavior as appropriate to the bad interpersonal environment, and these defenses prevent them from feeling alone and unworthy (Adler, 1990).

Families of Patients with Personality Disorders

Typically, the intrapsychic and the interpersonal components of psychopathology are inseparable in patients with personality disorders. These patients have important interpersonal problems, and family members remain significantly involved in these problems, even if the patient is over 30 years of age (Schulz et al., 1985). The complementary roles of the significant others in the negative behavior cycles of the patient with a personality disorder are often observed in family interviews (Villeneuve & Guttman, 1994). For example, with a borderline patient in a fusional relationship with one parent and still involved in a battle of separation, the reciprocal influence of both parties on the difficulty of separating and on the destructive behavior will become obvious. The active participation of both parties in the treatment usually accelerates the separation process (Villeneuve & Guttman, 1994).

Patients with personality disorders mystify their family and create significant stress with their outbursts of anger and their inability to see others as separate individuals with their own needs (Gunderson, Berkowitz, & Ruiz-Sancho, 1997). They seem unaware of the burden that they place on their family. This is particularly so for patients with narcissistic personality disorders. Narcissistic patients continuously feel personally injured and want others to confirm their worth. They tend to fly into rages when facing slight threats to self-esteem. Narcissistic parents often use their children as repositories of narcissistic gratification (Villeneuve & Guttman, 1994). They tend to form a collusive pathological pair with their partner or one of their children. When pairing occurs with a child, the latter is exposed to very negative interpersonal processes that prevent emotional development (Feldman & Guttman, 1984). The interpersonal boundaries being too thin, the parent may intrude upon the child with devalorization or pathological idealization.

The stress experienced by the families of personality-disordered individuals is usually ignored. The strong countertransference feelings that have been reported in psychotherapy with these patients are experienced on a daily basis by their families, such as feelings of inadequacy for not having done enough to respond to their insatiable demands. According to Gunderson and colleagues (1997), borderline patients are, for parents, the most difficult type of psychiatric problem to have in the family. The burden is greater than living with a member with a serious physical illness and for their offspring, greater than living with schizophrenic parents.

Studying newly referred psychiatric adult patients (137) with children up to 15 years of age (292), Rutter and Quinton (1984) found that having a parent with a conduct disorder was the single most significant factor in predicting psychopathology in the children. Almost half of these children showed a disturbance, more than twice the rate in children with a parent suffering from schizophrenia or an affective psychosis (21%).

Limitations of Individual Psychotherapy

To Horwitz and colleagues (1996), the borderline syndrome is made of heterogeneous patients who need an individualized psychotherapeutic approach. There is enough variation in the syndrome to allow the use of a variety of therapeutic modalities which are usually applied through a multimodal intervention (Paris, 1996). The clinician has to be pragmatic in the treatment of this condition and of other personality disorders and must be familiar with more than one approach.

Various types of psychotherapy have been tried, and there is evidence that psychodynamic psychotherapy is effective with some personality disorders patients (Gabbard, 1994), that is, those who have some capacity for insight and some degree of personality cohesion. There is some consensus, however, that explorative psychotherapy is of limited value in a large number of cases, and that regressive transference is often not constructive (Paris, 1996). Even if it is suitable, this creates a problem in large outpatient clinics with shortages of resources.

Cognitive–behavior therapy seems promising for treating personality disorders. Linehan and colleagues (1991), in controlled clinical trials of the cognitive–behavioral treatment of low-functioning borderlines, showed that this method can be modified to deal with specific problems such as noncompliance and parasuicidal behaviors. Patients treated with CBT for up to a year had a decrease of parasuicidal behavior, and were more likely to complete therapy than did control patients receiving the usual outpatient treatment (Linehan et al., 1991). It has to be noticed, however, that the treatment included one hour of individual psychotherapy and two and a half hours of group therapy each week.

The extreme difficulty in engaging these patients in treatment complicates the use of individual psychotherapy. In one study, Gunderson and colleagues (1989) found that over half of borderline personality disorder patients were early psychotherapy dropouts. The psychotherapy of personality disorders has become important, as there is a growing number of individuals with character pathology who are asking for help. The need for time-limited and economical treatments is obvious.

Characteristics of Interpersonal Treatment

The literature of the psychotherapeutic treatment of patients with personality disorders focuses almost exclusively on individual psychotherapy, especially on psychodynamic psychotherapy, and on these patients' subjective lives. Taking into account the general pessimism regarding their treatment and the fact that so many of these patients fail to respond to traditional approaches, it may be worth looking at the intervention from an interpersonal perspective. A group approach has been suggested by Segal and Weideman (1995) as part of a spectrum of interventions, usually as an adjunct to individual treatment. It may also worth exploring with conjoint therapy, especially with the most severe cases and individuals with personality disorders who are not motivated to obtain individual help but are causing distress to their significant others.

Conjoint or group therapy should be based on the same characteristics that have proven effective in individual psychotherapy of some personality disorders, particularly borderline personality disorder (Horwitz et al., 1996). These include using a flexible format and establishing a stable treatment framework with limit setting. In this way, the patient is provided with the structure and containment needed to develop a sense of self with limits. The structure becomes "a safe container of emotional turbulence and unrestrained action" (Horwitz et al., 1996, p. 137). However, a trusting relationship previously has to be established, and is a sine qua non condition to the efficacy of interpersonal treatment.

This structure, which is developed by the therapeutic system (the therapist and the family or group) should strengthen the patients' ego, forcing them to perceive their problem as internal and perhaps to feel pain. The therapeutic system should compel these patients to take responsibility for their actions and to respect the others in their lives. This could decrease their self-centered behavior. As pressure is put on the personality-disordered patients to contain themselves and to consider others, they may become more aware of others' feelings and the consequences of their maladaptive behavior (Budman, Cooley, Demby, & Koppenaal, 1996). This is particularly important for the narcissistic patients.

The work is usually done from the overt behavior toward the intra-psychic, from the outside to the inside. Thus, containing acting-out behavior, may be the first therapeutic step, and a prerequisite in dealing with other issues. If there is abuse or addiction, for example, this behavior has to be tackled first. In marital therapy for narcissistic couples, Lansky (1985) first addresses the marital partners' impulsive symptoms before focusing on other problems.

To establish a therapeutic structure, the therapist must provide strong leadership and prevent the usual negative interpersonal patterns. The therapists lend their reality to the family or group so that the members coalesce around this new perspective. The therapist also provides structure and containment as he or she bears and metabolizes the patient's distorted and acted-out affects for the other members. It is also important to focus on one problem at a time, as the patient with a personality disorder tends to dilute conflicts and get lost in arguments.

As suggested (Villeneuve & Guttman, 1994), the family or group therapist has to be responsive to the emotional needs of the patient with personality disorder and, at the same time, provide holding and limits, particularly to the patient with fragile ego and a low tolerance for frustration. Being responsive and active, which helps decrease the intensity of the transference, may be particularly suited for severe borderline patients who have primitive transference, in one-to-one psychotherapy (Roth, Stone, & Kibel, 1990). In fact, the active participation of the therapist and the other group or family members as real people not only provides containment, but also may decrease idealization and primitive defenses of splitting. This stance also may suit the narcissistically vulnerable individuals, who need personalized attention to meet their extreme craving for dependency.

The emphasis on structure can bring negative reactions from these hypersensitive patients, and they may leave therapy prematurely when the treatment does not go their way or when their position in the family or group is questioned. The therapist has to be sensitive to the patient, particularly when the patient's omnipotent defenses are confronted. As shown in the case of Mr. Harris, discussed in the next section, a balance is needed between empathizing and challenging, which is known to be effective in the individual treatment of narcissistically vulnerable individuals (Gunderson, 1984).

Countertransference issues, which frequently interfere with the necessary empathic response toward patients with personality disorders, can be handled more easily in conjoint or group therapy than in individual psychotherapy. For various reasons, such as the malleability of the therapeutic framework, the therapist has more leeway to master countertransference (see the techniques used with Mr. Harris). Cotherapy is also very useful to deal with these patients' resistance to change and the intense negative feelings that they instill.

Conjoint and group therapy with personality disorders requires a good theoretical and empirical background, as well as flexibility in its implementation. To be flexible, the treatment, for example, may shift back and forth between individual and conjoint (or group) therapy, depending upon the evolution of the intervention. If one approach is at an impasse, or if the patient wants to leave therapy prematurely, the therapist may shift to another approach. This flexible format could be used more easily when the therapist has a range of skills to implement both the individual and the interpersonal treatment. In this way, stalemates occuring in the treatment may be better dealt with and compliance may be increased. Selective referral is also possible, different therapists doing separate approaches.

Conjoint Therapy

As personality disorders are assumed to be related to environmental failure leading to deprivation or fixation, some resistant patients initially may respond better to a change in the relational environment that they have helped develop. In any case, families of patients with borderline and other personality disorders are often more motivated to seek help than the patient. They at least need to understand the illness. Because they are familiar with feeling responsible for the patient, this pathological attitude can be used therapeutically and then reversed to make the patient feel more responsible.

A cohesive approach is needed from the start with the development of a working alliance with all the people involved and a strong therapeutic structure. The family interactions are monitored and the patient's usual negative interpersonal patterns and constant attempts to modify the structure are prevented. Rules are set in order to restrict negative behavior during the sessions. The therapist has to be in firm control of what goes on during each session, and may have to intervene frequently (Villeneuve & Guttman, 1994). For example, if members are getting lost in arguments, and chaos and confusion prevail, the therapist may decide to give one the floor to talk while the others will listen and will be prevented from intruding. Spatial interventions, such as modifying the seating arrangement, using a one-way mirror, or seeing only one family subsystem for part of the session, are helpful techniques to keep the therapeutic structure constant. Between-session contact, such as phone calls, even may have to be controlled.

The consistency of the therapeutic frame and the limit setting usually help the family to become the holding structure for the resistant or otherwise difficult patient who is disturbing his significant others. The family members are used as a therapeutic lever. Without resorting to negative behavior, other family members have to learn how to verbalize the impact that the patient's maladaptive behavior has on them. They also have to set limits to curtail the omnipotent feelings that often underlie acting-out behavior, and render this behavior ego-alien. Clarifications and confrontations made by the participants and the therapist can be a powerful way to structure and tackle distortions and the pathological syntonic defenses underlying the character pathology.

Again, referring to the case of Mr. Harris, the therapist may occasionally exert the containing function while doing individual work with the patient in the presence of the other participants. Appropriate ways to handle pathological behavior can then be modeled. Being calm as well as emotionally available, the therapist may demonstrate how it is possible to be empathic and holding even when the patient is difficult.

A strong therapeutic structure may be necessary to tackle the power related a chronic physical condition or a psychological ailment in a family member with personality disorder (see the case of Mrs. Clark in chapter 6). The secondary gains often attached to these conditions can indeed benefit this patient whose ailment is accompanied with a personality disorder. These individuals may become increasingly self-centered, passive, and dependent on the other family members. They may tyrannize significant others with their condition, demanding full attention and constant care. The phenomenon is often present in cases of depression of Axis 1 type complicated with personality disorders.

Some restructuring may then be feasible. Restructuring often means dealing with the structural problems present in these families such as coalition, triangulation of one member, enmeshment, and isolation. Whether the patient is a parent or an adult child still living with the parents, the intergenerational boundaries are usually diffused in these families. By strengthening the parental subsystem the power hierarchy is reestablished with the parents at the top. If restructuring is effective and confusion has decreased, dealing with other issues such as improving communication and delineating personal and family problems may then become possible. A summary of the treatment of a parent with a personality disorder follows. It is a complicated case, which could well represent the type of problems often faced in clinical settings.

Bryan Hams, 8 years old and an only child, acted domineering and aggressively to his peers and was constantly seeking adult attention. He had been seen in individual therapy for a year and his mother met with the same therapist from time to time. Bryan held the balance of power in his family, which could hardly be treated in individual psychotherapy. As the boy's improvement was minimal, the Harris family was finally referred for conjoint therapy. Family tension was unexpectedly high and Bryan was triangulated between his warring parents. The mother and the son were in constant friction, and the father reacted by taking his son's side and overprotecting him.

The family's traditional roles were reversed: Mrs. Harris was the breadwinner, while Mr. Harris took care of the household and worked part time as a salesman. He hardly had any clients as his interpersonal difficulties, such as extreme irritability and aggressive stance, prevented him from functioning adequately. Mr. Harris always had been a loner and he started to drink in his teens. From Bryan's birth, he invested heavily in his son and made sure he was treated differently than himself as a child. For example, he could not tolerate his wife's taking an ascendency over the boy.

Strategies had to be used to engage Mr. Harris into treatment. Unmotivated to seek help for himself or his family, he agreed to come to therapy to help his son. After months of conjoint therapy that focused on strengthening the parental subsystem, Bryan was finally detriangulated. The couple's problems became more amenable to treatment and the parents were seen in marital therapy. They were stuck in a circle of aversive behavior and the therapist had to intervene frequently to prevent this pathological process.

It came out during marital therapy that Mr. Harris was drinking heavily at night, which the previous therapist had not known. This was a family secret. According to the parents, Bryan did not know about his father's drinking behavior, but admitted later that he knew and had used it to get his way and get things from his father. When drunk, Mr. Harris desperately tried to communicate with his wife and get her attention. Mrs. Harris responded to her husband's wish for communication by withdrawing from him and spending more time at work which, in turn, increased Mr. Harris' drinking and his proximity to Bryan.

During sessions, Mr. Harris continually blamed his wife. Attempts to clarify communication were unproductive. He could not follow basic ground rules for adequate communications. When his wife was talking, he could not stop interrupting, and denied whatever she said. He was completely unable to acknowledge his wife's own perspective and needs. Video play back was used to help him gain some distance. Feeling threatened in his position and no longer able to downplay his drinking, Mr. Harris resorted to threatening his spouse. He also felt irritated by the therapist's interventions, and thought the therapist was siding with his wife. Mr. Harris' relationship to the therapist, as well as his wife's firm decision to hold her ground, prevented further deterioration and the maintenance of a therapeutic space. Unable to deny his heavy drinking any more and feeling supported, Mr. Harris finally joined AA, which quickly sparked a cycle of positive behavior in the family. Concurrent marital therapy went on for another year.

Mrs. Harris' role in their marital difficulties was dealt with, in particular her passive-aggressive attitude toward her husband and her difficulty getting close to people. In the meantime, Mr Harris' psychopathology became more and more evident. He revealed that he felt trapped in his relationships and forced to remain distant, and had an inability to be empathic. He had been raised very strictly by his mother who was not attuned to his needs. He learned to rely only on himself, and alcohol and drugs became an alternative to him. With the therapist's help, both Mr. and Mrs. Harris became more aware of their relationship pattern, their individual vulnerabilities, and those of their partner. Mr. Harris threatened to end therapy many times. To unblock his resistance and to save the treatment, empathic restructuring was provided by individual work done with him in the presence of his wife. At other times, marital therapy was not possible, and he was seen alone for some periods of the treatment.

The reader will notice that Mr. Harris was not bothered by his problematic behavior, like many patients with personality disorders, and that, in the first phase of his treatment, individual psychotherapy was not feasible. The presence of many participants and the malleability of the therapeutic framework allowed flexibility in the treatment with the use of a variety of methods and techniques, making his participation possible and eventually leading him to join an AA group.

This case also highlights some characteristics of interpersonal treatment in general. The therapist has to be active and structuring, stepping in to prevent escalation and to ensure a stable and safe therapeutic atmosphere. Mr. Harris was strategically placed in situations in which he had to perceive his problems as internal as well as the consequences of his maladaptive behavior. The therapeutic structure was firm but acceptable to Mr. Harris. The therapist was empathic to him and responsive to his emotional needs, which probably saved the therapeutic alliance. Some of these therapist's characteristics (being active, structuring, and responsive) are known to make psychotherapy effective (see chapter 1).

In the interpersonal treatment of patients with personality disorders, the therapists have many ways of tackling problems as they appear in therapy. In this way, the intervention remains multimodal and tailored to the patient as recommended by Horwitz and colleagues (1996). As in the case of Mr. Harris, the participation of the index patient may vary.

Audiovisual methods, such as the use of video play back or a one-way mirror, are useful with patients with personality disorders. For example, the attention-seeking or manipulative patient may be asked to be an observer for the entire session while the other family members participate actively. Such a technique allows distancing from problems, which is an important issue in psychotherapy, especially for patients with personality disorders. Even though techniques do not count much in psychotherapy efficacy (see chapter 1), they have a structuring effect and help bring new perspectives. This is not negligible in patients with personality disorders and their families.

As discussed in chapter 3, when patients do not see the problem as theirs but as belonging to another family, they may be strategically involved in conjoint therapy by explaining to them that their participation is necessary to change the other (as was the case with Mr. Harris). With patients refusing treatment altogether, their significant others may come with them or, if necessary, force them to come by whatever means they have at their disposal. Their relatives even may come alone so as to learn to set limits or other ways to alleviate their suffering caused by the patient. This finally may bring the patient into treatment.

As in individual psychotherapy, conjoint therapy with personality-disordered patients is unpredictable. The intervention may be lengthy, with no clear-cut results. This may appear obsolete in the era of the quick-fix approach to psychotherapy. It is no surprise that not many of these families are taken into treatment, even though it is worth the effort to try new alternatives as part of an integrated and flexible approach.

Group Therapy

Group therapy is not widely used with personality disorders, even though this setting provides excellent conditions for treating this psychopathology (Linehan et al., 1991). According to Budman, Cooley, and colleagues (1996), the relevance of treating patients with personality disorders in time-limited group therapy stems from the characteristic and persistent difficulty of these patients to relate to others and their lack of internal structure, which quickly surface in groups.

Group interventions allow the dilution of the transference, as the patient has more room to relate to the therapist due to the presence of other members. The group also provides peer pressure, and a stronger reality orientation and boundary definition based on social interactions, compared to individual interventions (Budman, Cooley, et al., 1996). Clarkin, Marziali, & Munroe-Blum (1991) mentioned other advantages to the use of group therapy with borderline personality disorder patients: an ability to accept feedback more easily from other patients than from the therapist, individual psychotherapy too costly for them, and a shortage of trained psychotherapists.

The group approaches most frequently used in treating personality disorders are based on Yalom's (1995) interpersonal group model and on object relations theory. The main characteristics of the approach and the role of the therapist as described above are similar in both group and conjoint therapy. In their model for time-effective group psychotherapy for patients with personality disorders, Budman, Cooley, and colleagues (1996) have discussed these characteristics:

1. interpersonal focus using the here-and-now, the confrontation of these patients' disturbing behavior and the rehearsal for change;
2. the therapist's active structuring, with limit setting and rules to provide external control;
3. focusing on group interaction and process as curative factors;
4. time limits; and
5. encouraging strengths and responsibility.

Most types of patients with personality disorders are suitable for group therapy (Budman, Cooley, et al., 1996). This therapeutic modality has been reported to be particularly useful in treating borderline and narcissistic personality disorders, offering opportunities for support and confrontation within the group (Roth et al., 1990; see also the clinical vignette in chapter 5). Group therapy, however, is usually suited to the more functional end of the personality disorder continuum. According to Budman, Cooley, and colleagues (1996), severely-impaired patients are difficult to manage and may impede adequate group functioning. Furthermore, most group therapies of patients with personality disorders focus on short-term interventions, while these patients require long-term treatment. Group therapists argue, however, that a time-limited intervention could be one episode in an intermittent treatment over a long period of time, with no responsibility for "curing" the patient. Spitz (1996) suggests sequential brief therapy from time to time as not only psychologically sound, but more economical than years of ongoing individual psychotherapy.

Efficacy of Conjoint and Group Therapy

As presented in chapter 4, conjoint therapy has been shown to be an effective treatment of serious mental disorders, including personality disorders, when combined with other therapeutic modalities. The effectiveness of conjoint therapy has also been evidenced with both adolescent and adult drug abusers. In addition, some studies suggest that conjoint therapy is more cost effective than alternative treatment for adolescent and adult drug abusers (Pinsof & Wynne, 1995). The same was also found in family-involved therapy for alcoholism.

Reviewing the outcome literature on group therapy for patients with personality disorders, Budman, Cooley, and colleagues (1996) concluded that group therapy is quite effective with a heterogeneous range of personality disorders, and may be more effective than individual psychotherapy. The effective use of group therapy with borderline patients has been well substantiated by research (Marziali & Munroe-Blum, 1994). Budman, Demby, and colleagues (1996) reported the results of their own outcome study in a time-limited (18 months), interpersonally-oriented group therapy of 49 outpatients, most of whom were diagnosed as having personality disorders. There was a significant reduction in personality-disorder criteria in pre-and postgroup. Subjects reported substantial changes in self-esteem, symptomatology, and diagnosability on Axis II. There was, however, no control group with a no-treatment sample used.

☐ Other Chronic Mental Illness

Therapeutic work with the families of chronically-ill psychiatric patients is rare, even though there are many reasons to involve these families in the treatment. People with schizophrenia and other psychiatric patients may need a person as an auxiliary ego, especially if their condition becomes chronic, that is, they suffer from a severe and persistent mental disorder that hampers their functional capacities in relation to their daily life. Focusing only on the patient would mean expecting that the chronically-ill person to be able to cope alone with his illness. Individual treatment must, therefore, be supported by interventions, possibly including the family and community services.

The active involvement of significant others is important in the treatment of people with schizophrenia for other reasons (Procter & Pieczora, 1993):

1. Failure to involve significant others leads to longer admission periods, more relapses and increased hostility from their families.
2. Treatment is complicated by the fact that up to 57% of the schizophrenic patients also have an Axis II personality disorder.
3. Because of their need to keep a distance from people, people with schizophrenia may shut down so that significant communication with the therapist may have to be done through a close relative.

At follow-up visits to the psychiatrist for medication and support, it is beneficial to see schizophrenic patients with one or more of the people who are close to them, for part of or for the whole interview. As reported by Procter and Pieczora (1993), because of their difficulty communicating and their lack of insight, relying only on what the patients report about themselves and others may be misleading. Psychotic patients may hide their delusions, and their peculiar behavior may be known only to the people who are close to them. Furthermore, as people with schizophrenia are noncompliant with medication (48% within the first year and up to 74% within the first two years), another person may have to monitor their medication (Corrigan, Lieberman, & Engel, 1990).

Families as Primary Caregivers

Psychiatric hospitalization in Western countries is geared to eliminate acute symptoms. Often little is done to help the family understand the psychotic patient and help prepare to take the family member home. To Hatfield and Lefley (1993), the failure of community treatment programs to replace the total environment of the hospital by providing assistance and support to chronic mental patients and their families has contributed to making the families the primary caregivers, a task for which they are often ill prepared.

At the beginning of the treatment, and in their first contacts with mental health workers, families are usually very involved. But they often get the message that only professionals can handle mentally ill patients and families are blocked from participating in the hospital treatment. Nor are professionals trained to help families, and the hospital setting is usually not suited for this task. Families of the mentally ill are in great need of information and practical advice concerning the illness and how to cope with the patient (Lefley, 1996). They may have inaccurate assumptions about the nature of the illness, its causes, and its evolution; they also may be puzzled by the florid symptoms of schizophrenia.

The existential impact of chronic mental illness on these families is not adequately acknowledged by mental health workers. These families need support as the care of the mental patients can be an enormous burden. Patients may need a person present at all times, as they may feel unable to tolerate being alone. The caregivers can feel imprisoned by their obligation to the patient, and may be unable to have a life of their own (Backlar, 1994). They often need help in dealing with the difficulty of caring for the patient, while preventing his regression.

The effects of living with a mentally ill patient can be overwhelming when one of the parents decompensates. The children may witness the progressive deterioration of the patient, throwing them into a strange world. Moreover, the restabilization period following a psychotic episode usually takes place at home. This can be a difficult period for the family. The patient is not ready to go back to work and may demand a lot of attention. Family members also may feel bewildered by the remission–recurrence phase of the illness, and think the patient is not doing his or her best. To complicate the situation, people with chronic schizophrenia have problems tolerating, modulating, and expressing affects. Anger may be particularly difficult to manage. These patients often keep their feelings inside until they explode.

Families Are Still Blamed or Ignored

The blame and neglect of the family of the mentally-ill is not new. Historically, the asylum was built partly because the family was seen as being detrimental to the mental patient. Psychoanalytic theories such as the "schizophrenogenic mother," and family theories, such as the "double bind," consolidated these beliefs.

The importance currently given to biological factors in the etiology and management of major mental illness has changed this picture somewhat. However, even though psychoanalytic and family theories are only of historical value nowadays, they continue to have a tremendous impact on the treatment of the families of the chronically-ill, and many clinicians are still influenced by them (Lefley, 1996). These theories have contributed to create a distance between families and clinicians and might prevent the development of trust and cooperation, which is so important in schizophrenia. The family is still subtly blamed or ignored. These clinicians' attitudes are well summarized by Anderson, Hogarty, and Reiss (1980):

> Families are often ignored or mistreated by mental health professionals, or at best given sympathy without direction [. . .] In many cases, whatever contact is made with the family contains the implication that they are to blame for the patient's problems, further stimulating guilt, pain, and potentially leading to the family's withdrawal from the treatment system (p. 495).

Even though in the past 20 years programs have been developed to help the families of chronic psychiatric patients, research shows that families are greatly dissatisfied with the way they are treated (Hanson & Rapp, 1992).

A Family-Oriented Approach

In practice, not much is done to help the family of the patient with a chronic mental illness, even though it has been shown that family work with schizophrenia is often better than individual intervention (see Falloon et al., 1982). It is more cost effective in a variety of areas, including the need for hospitalization, the delay of dependence on institutional care, and a decrease in the level of symptoms. The family is irreplaceable in the care of mental patients, nobody else can have such an ongoing interest.

The family-oriented approach emphasizes the importance of supporting the natural system of the patients and of other people who care for them and validating their negative experience (Hatfield & Lefley, 1993). The term "family therapy," which carries the notion that there is a family pathology, may sound inappropriate in dealing with the family of the seriously-ill psychiatric patient. To Wynne, McDaniel, and Weber (1987), family therapy may easily imply that the family is the patient and this may be perceived as an added blow, considering that the family is already traumatized.

The family was sometimes forced to attend sessions with no excuses allowed for not having the whole family present. NAMI has bitterly criticized family therapists for trying to change the family dynamic rather than giving information and advice concerning the care of the schzophrenic family member. The notion of "schizophrenic families" is now replaced by "families with a schizophrenic member" (Wynne et al., 1987).

Wynne and his collaborators (1987) have suggested the term "family consultation" in the first phase of helping families with a psychiatrically-ill member. According to these authors, this term seems to be more acceptable to families, as it conveys to the families that this is initially an evaluative process and that their cooperation is sought. The meeting with the family (or the other people with whom the patient lives) allows the therapist to gather information, to assess options after initial contact, and to develop an alliance with the family. Family consultations may help, especially when there is a treatment deadlock. Intermittent consultations and ongoing support groups also seem effective for families with a member with a chronic illness (Wynne et al., 1987).

Occasionally, there is still a place for classical conjoint therapy with these families. Either the whole family or a few individuals closely involved with the patient may be seen. The theoretical framework then used is generally based on adaptation. The relatives may be helped to see how they may be ineffective in dealing with their sick member. The problem of limit setting, for example, is frequent in these families—members either being overinvolved or not dealing at all with limits. Dealing with this type of problem can also be discussed in relatives' groups (psychoeducational or self-help groups). It may be worth reiterating that the most effective interventions with the families of the mentally ill are usually educational or consultation-focused, and do not correspond to classical modes of conjoint therapy (Hatfield & Lefley, 1993).

Psychoeducational Groups

A fair number of research has shown a positive correlation between the expressed emotions (EE) in the family and the recurrence of schizophrenia. When the relatives are rated high on EE, it seems more likely that the patient will have relapses (Anderson et al., 1980). The relatives who express low EE cope with abnormal behavior by ignoring it and by emphasizing positive behavior. Those high in EE are upset and angry with the patient's problematic behavior, and this has often become their only possible reaction. They may be hostile and often overinvolved, or else they give up. These findings led to the development of the psychoeducational approach for families with a schizophrenic member.

Psychoeducational intervention centers around decreasing the patient's vulnerability to stress by reducing the family's expression of negative feelings (criticality and hostility). The families are usually seen in groups. Based on Anderson's (1980) and Falloon's (1982) work, families with a schizophrenic member are taught that they can play a role in protecting the patient from relapsing by reducing stresses and by developing problem-solving abilities. It is assumed that, following the intervention, the difficult periods that will inevitably happen will be dealt with and buffeted by the family.

Education about schizophrenia is an important component of psychoeducation. After learning that there is a biochemical defect in schizophrenia, relatives may feel less guilty. As they acquire knowledge about the cognitive and emotional deficits of schizophrenics, they may be able to better distinguish between symptoms and behavior that is under the patient's control. Psychoeducation minimizes the negative effects of illness on others and is a low-cost, mental health promotion. McFarlane and colleagues (1995) reported a cost-effectiveness ratio of $34 of inpatient costs saved for every dollar spent on psychoeducational programs. Even though education about mental illness and management issues are very important, most centers do not provide it, and this can hardly be accomplished in traditional individual treatment.

The assumption of high EE in families with schizophrenia has been criticized lately. These families may once again feel blamed, as they may be perceived as being either critical or overinvolved with the patient. Lefley (1996) who has written extensively on the subject, has expressed doubts about the causal relationship between EE and the relapse rate of schizophrenia. She argues that the preponderance of the literature shows that, throughout the world, families with a schizophrenic member generally have a low EE, and she recommends that EE research be concerned with the course and outcome of schizophrenia, not the etiology.

The relationship between EE and relapsing is difficult to interpret. Lefley (1996) suggests that high levels of EE may be related to relatives reacting to very difficult behavior on the part of the patient. Still, the psychoeducational approach appears to be most in line with families' wishes for help vis à vis mental illness, and is a necessary care component for patients with severe mental illness (North et al., 1998). The most recent approach (see Hatfield & Lefley, 1993) emphasizes a holistic view, and sees the family as a key resource. Within a learning/ educational approach, the clinician is pragmatic and supportive, and shares power over decision making with families of the mentally ill. Finally, family involvement has to be part of a comprehensive program, which should also include residential rehabilitation facilities and self-help groups.

Efficacy of Psychoeducational Groups

Anderson's (1980) and Falloon's (1982) work showing the efficacy of the psychoeducational approach have been confirmed by many other studies. Reviewing the research literature on family psychoeducational interventions in schizophrenia, Goldstein and Miklowitz (1995) found "convincing evidence" demonstrating the superiority of these interventions plus medication over medication alone (p. 372). Over two-year periods, family interventions are more effective than individual approaches in delaying relapses and improving social functioning.

CHAPTER 8

Integration

Brought about by socioeconomic and scientific forces, an important trend in the field of psychotherapy is the move toward the rationalization and integration of approaches. A single theoretical model may be easier to handle and give the clinician a feeling of confidence, but it cannot suit the diversity of clinical problems. To help understand the integration of conjoint and group therapy, some general aspects of this integration first will be discussed and some models of integrating conjoint and group therapy will be presented.

☐ General Considerations

According to Beutler and Clarkin (1990), the current threat as to whether psychotherapy should be conducted, and under which conditions, is so strong that the traditional rivalry between opposing schools has been replaced by an alliance that may create a significant change in the practice of psychotherapy. The radical accent on differences has slowly given way to synthesizing the knowledge from various schools and integrating approaches. The false dichotomy that often exists between biological treatment and psychotherapy can also be attenuated when the intervention is integrative. The majority of therapists have become integrative in their orientation (Lambert & Bergin, 1994).

In a survey reported by Norcross and Newman (1992), the combination of individual and conjoint or group therapy is seen as being within the boundaries of integration by more than 80% of clinicians. Many foresee the rise of flexible formats, such as concurrent or sequential combinations of individual, group, or conjoint treatment. To deal with shrinking resources, the integration of group and family interventions to individual approaches present an interesting alternative.

Conjoint therapy is poorly integrated with other therapeutic modalities, even though there is a historical association between this modality and individual interventions in the treatment of the most severe disorders, such as schizophrenia and anorexia nervosa. In the case of group therapy, however, significant efforts have been made to integrate this modality with individual approaches (see Yalom, 1995).

The research literature reviewed in this book has shown that conjoint and group approaches are applicable to most psychiatric conditions when combined with individual treatment. Conjoint and group therapies are effective as adjuncts to individual treatment in multimodal interventions with severe mental illness such as schizophrenia and personality disorder. Feldman (1992), who has written extensively on the topic, argues that this type of integration can greatly enhance the treatment of these conditions.

In schizophrenia, for example, the psychoeducational approach is a very useful adjunct to medication and support. We have seen that adding psychoeducation to individual treatment is cost effective, as it improves the patient's functionality, decreases relapses, and assists with compliance with medication. Also, as discussed in chapter 7, patients with personality disorders usually need a multimodal approach, often including individual, group, or family treatment. Axis I disorders, which are often present in these patients, do not respond well to standard individual treatment. Moreover, in treating substance abuse and eating disorders, combined treatments are more effective than single-model interventions. For example, adolescents with anorexia nervosa respond better to treatment when conjoint therapy is part of the intervention (see chapter 6). The age of the patient also influences integration. Younger and older people usually respond better to an integrative approach involving the patient's significant others than to single interventions alone.

Furthermore, it is more and more evident that current mental health care programs, in order to decrease costs, are pressuring for accountability, and are fostering the use of integrative programs to suit a broader range of patients and to improve psychotherapy. This book attempts to show how conjoint and group approaches particularly well suit the philosophy of managed care or any other cost-containment mental health care program. They should be in the forefront of mental health care reforms, but this is a challenge to the tradition of once-a-week individual psychotherapy. It is well documented that these modalities are effective, lend themselves easily to brief intervention, and are economical. Brief interventions save available clinical time and reach more patients.

Conjoint therapy is usually brief for various reasons, such as the family, the members' natural resource system, is activated in therapy and family members carry the therapy experience into their daily interactions, which increases the possibility for change (Combrinck-Graham, 1996). Many current conjoint therapeutic orientations, such as Minuchin's structural approach (Nichols & Minuchin, 1999), are brief and goal-oriented.

Group therapy and self-help groups are also of increasing importance in regard to managed care or any other cost-containment programs. We are entering into the third age of group therapy, which is mostly based on economic and scientific reasons, and contributes to orient that therapeutic modality toward briefer and less expensive interventions. Dies (1993) has shown that group therapy is more economical than individual psychotherapy, and that for many emotional problems, it is just as effective. Stone (1996) reaches the same conclusion about groups for maintaining functioning in patients with chronic psychiatric illness.

Throughout this book, comparative cost-effectiveness research pertaining to psychotherapy, when available, is reported. For example, Bray and Jouriles (1995) substantiated the cost effectiveness of marital therapy, showing it is far below the alternatives. Systemic thinking brings an important dimension to cost effectiveness as the other family members and institutions with which the patient interacts should be included in the evaluation of the treatment costs (Pinsof & Wynne, 1995). In treating a psychotic mother, for example, it is necessary to look at the use of services not only by the mother, but also by her spouse and children.

☐ Some Models of Integration

Following Schacht's (1984) models of psychotherapy integration, below are some models of integrating conjoint or group psychotherapy with individual psychotherapeutic modalities. These models may help bypass many of the limitations of single approaches, and may better fit the variety of presenting problems.

1. Conjoint or group therapy and individual therapy are complementary. They usually deal with separate problems in the same individual. Using both orientations, a synergistic effect can be obtained, the two therapies producing a result superior to that obtained by either therapy on its own. As spelled out by Feldman (1992), the advantages of each approach may increase those of the other, while their limitations may be decreased by the other's strengths. The combined format of individual and group therapy has been shown by empirical research to be an effective strategy for a variety of patients (Fuhriman & Burlingame, 1994).

Individual therapy may help the course of conjoint or group therapy, and the reverse also may be true. On the one hand, a desired change in conjoint or group therapy may be blocked by an intrapsychic conflict, and individual psychotherapy may be added to tackle this difficulty. Conjoint therapy, on the other hand, may enhance individual therapy, family members, for example, supporting compliance with medication or sobriety. A patient may be seen individually for his neurotic problems while conjoint or group therapy may be added as a specific intervention tailored to a specific problem (see the case of Paula below).

Looking at the stage of change as a basic element of the intervention is an interesting way to explore this model of integration. It is logical to first use the simplest, most cost-effective and least-intrusive approach, such as dealing with obvious behaviors. This is typical of CBT and some interpersonal therapies. On the other hand, a patient may have given up an old pattern in individual therapy but still may be unable to initiate a new pattern on his own. An action-oriented modality such as CBT, group therapy, or conjoint therapy then may be more helpful.

The case of Ann described in chapter 5 illustrates the use of sequential therapies. This woman was seen first in individual psychotherapy, and group therapy was added later. Both therapists felt the combination of the two therapeutic modalities facilitated and hastened change. This type of intervention may not be sufficiently explored. There are, however, some research studies pertaining to this subject. Interviewing 42 randomly selected patients, 2–14 years after termination of group therapy, Malan and associates (1976) found a very strong positive correlation between positive outcome from psychoanalytic group psychotherapy and previous individual psychoanalytic psychotherapy. Yalom (1995) also reported that individual psychotherapy is sometimes needed first for the fragile patient to use the group effectively.

This combination probably works better when the two psychotherapies are of the same orientation. This was the case with Ann in chapter 5. Experiences with a sequence of psychotherapies of different orientations has not been always positive. Some patients who had been previously in long-term psychoanalytic psychotherapy found it difficult to adapt to nonanalytic conjoint or group therapy.

As discussed previously, the intervention should also be done first at the level where the system shows some elasticity and not too much resistance. The choice should be based, as well, on the principle of least psychopathology, and using as many of the resources available in the patient's interpersonal milieu, without resorting too quickly to specialized services. This is very important in terms of cost saving, which gives an edge to interpersonal psychotherapy.

> Paula, a obese 19-year-old girl, was referred for suicidal ideations and poor social skills. She was the oldest of three siblings and the only girl. The family screening revealed a lot of unresolved and unexpressed tension within the family, especially between the parents, with the father's progressive estrangement from his wife and family. The mother's emotional problems and unmet needs were manifested through somatizations, periods of untreated depression and periodic acting-out behavior when she left home for hours without telling anybody where she was. Because of the family situation, Paula had taken over a good part of the household responsibilities very early on. She was, however, constantly criticized by her mother while remaining dependent and insecurely attached to her. At the time of the referral, though, the mother had become more empathic toward her daughter and was motivated to help her.
>
> When assessed individually, Paula appeared resourceful but overly mature for her age. She looked very depressed with symptoms of major depression. She was also constantly worrried about her mother and the rest of the family. She had a poor self-image, felt shy, awkward, and unable to cope with her peers. Besides schooling, she had very little social activities and had no friends. She minimally responded to drug treatment but enjoyed supportive therapy. She remained, however, very enmeshed into the family problem. So conjoint therapy (mother–daughter) was added to her ongoing individual treatment.

This dyad was selected for many reasons: the mother was playing an important role in the maintenance of Paula's problems; both women were motivated to seek conjoint help, which proved that this family subsystem was showing some elasticity; conjoint therapy meant a brief intervention, using the resources available in the patient's interpersonal environment.

> To help them give up their old interactional patterns, their common problems were translated into concrete interpersonal conflicts and interpersonal outcomes. The intervention had to be brief and focused, as the therapist and the two women each had limited time available. Realistic goals were set. They quickly responded to an approach based on exploration and understanding of their past and present relationship in regard to their interpersonal conflicts. In an atmosphere of empathy, their respective experience was validated, which decreased their mutual blaming and their guilt.

Through the integration of individual and conjoint treatment, Paula learned to set her own limits which helped her individuation. However, Paula was still very shy and socially awkward. She had given up old patterns and now had to try out new ways, but she had difficulty moving ahead. Paula was encouraged to go out to meet friends, but she found all kinds of excuses to stay home. Unable to socialize and to cope with peers, Paula became more passive and sad. The treatment plan had to be changed. Integrating an action-oriented behavioral approach to deal with her social inhibition seemed logical. Group therapy, which is particularly effective to deal with people presenting socialization problems, was offered.

She joined a social skills group, while individual psychotherapy was continued until she was well engaged in the group intervention. A safe place specifically designed to provide a testing ground for exposure to her fears and inhibitions was then provided. This brief group experience (10 sessions) was not enough, but Paula was moving toward a better social adaption.

2. Following Schacht's second model of integration, the combination of two psychotherapies may lead to an emergent therapeutic method. Using the strength of two psychotherapeutic orientations, such as the psychodynamic or the existential and the interpersonal, and their unique active ingredients, may produce a greater efficacy. An emergent therapeutic method is developed when family and group therapists see members individually, explore historical material in groups, and use experiential and action-oriented techniques (see the case below).

Within the second model of integration, therapists have integrated a variety of methods and techniques tailored to a continuum of problems, responding better to an integrative approach than insular psychotherapies. This goes along with Lambert's and Bergin's (1994) findings, that good therapists routinely used a variety of interventions associated with disparate orientations. Group therapists (see Leszcz, 1996) often integrate psychodynamic, existential, interpersonal, and cognitive–behavioral elements, capitalizing on the forces of each. Group members may analyze the historical context of their symptoms, examine their subjective experience of alienation, understand how they participate to maintenance of their interpersonal difficulties, and practice new skills (Leszcz, 1996).

The use of this model of integration may create or maintain intense emotional moments, some sort of experiential confrontations that foster perceptual and emotional shifts of the people in therapy. Combining psychodynamic, interpersonal, and experiential elements through ideas, affects, interaction, space, and body language may, for example, help move from hostile verbal exchanges between family or group members to reaching basic relational conflicts. This happened with Jason, the adolescent whose depression and acting-out was described in chapter 6.

> In the second session with Jason and his father, sculpting (a spatial representation of relationships) was used to reduce the hostile blaming of the father, who felt rejected by his son while being unable to listen to his pleas for help. Asked to place his father and himself in a way that would characterize their relationship, Jason portrayed his father as being angry at him and pushing him down on the floor. Both felt very uncomfortable about this sculpting. Jason was then asked to make a sculpting to represent how he would ideally like his relationship to his father to be. This brought about an intense emotional moment. Jason placed his father beside him, his arm around his son's shoulders, both walking in the same direction. The father started to cry, hugging his son close to him, and saying he wished he would have done this more often, as his own father had never hugged him.
>
> Interactions had moved from the father's blaming Jason to a new level of functioning. Jason's disclosing his deep feelings toward his father broke his father's firm conviction that his son harbored negative feelings toward him. The therapist used this therapeutic momentum to relabel Jason's problem and help both father and son focus on their respective feelings of abandonment. This eventually led to a climate of empathy and forgiveness. The father's expression of his own vulnerability led to compassion from his son, as he understood his father's hostility better. The following sessions were also structured to use the opening brought about by these sculptings.

This case also illustrates the malleability of conjoint and group therapy, allowing the clinician to be creative in using Gestalt techniques to improve communications between two family members. That integrative approach suited both the adolescent and his father, and was probably as effective and more cost-saving than traditional intervention requiring two therapists, one for the symptomatic boy and one for the father. The approach was tailored to the specific therapeutic needs of the two family members. As discussed before, it was also a simple and natural approach, using the resources available in the adolescent's milieu.

9
CHAPTER

Conclusion

The human element of psychotherapy may be more important than ever to counteract some of the negative effects of today's scientific and technical treatments. There can be no psychiatry without psychotherapy. Besides its specificity as an intervention, psychotherapy provides guidelines and daily support for the clinicians in their attitudes toward the patient, ensuring the efficacy of other interventions.

Even though in the United States, in particular, the forces of the marketplace are influencing what type of psychotherapy is going to be practiced, making patients and their families consumers with input in the selection and evaluation of the treatments offered, psychotherapy is unlikely to be eliminated, as it is both profitable and cost effective. Psychotherapy fulfills the requirements set by the cost reduction mandate of the current health systems of Western countries and is in line with the belief that treatment whose effectiveness has not been proven should not be paid for.

Psychotherapists are concerned about their roles in the health care reform that is taking place. Many find it difficult to adapt to the use of shorter forms of interventions, whether individual, conjoint, or group psychotherapy. Balance is needed, however, in the practice of psychotherapy. On the one hand, a psychotherapist who is too innovative may rely on fads and become clinically ineffective. Innovations must be evaluated to prevent eclectism and excess. A too-orthodox psychotherapist, on the other hand, whose assumptions and methods are not open to change, may develop dogmatism and repetitive dullness.

To get away from ideology and to bring change to psychotherapy practice, however, is very difficult. Psychotherapeutic modalities have developed into complex self-sustaining systems, which are not easy to change. As a transference-focused intervention, open-ended psycho-dynamic psychotherapy is more limited in its adaptability to change, precisely because the therapist's position can hardly change compared with other psychotherapies. Mental health workers have, however, a social responsibility to provide services to the general population and not only to a privileged group. Still, the practice and the teaching of the psychodynamic model must remain active in the clinical setting. This model is a necessary alternative to biological psychiatry.

There is now a multiplicity of effective treatments and ways to deal with psychological suffering. Psychotherapists must remain open to new ideas, which may lead to better psychotherapeutic alternatives. The traditional and somewhat effective way has been to focus almost exclusively on the individual. Psychotherapy, however, has to become more multifaceted and integrative. Focusing on the constellation of patients and people close to them, and placing a greater part of the intervention on groups and community support systems, such as self-help groups, are good alternatives and refreshing ways of conceptualizing mental health care delivery.

The advantages of conjoint and group-related interventions have been emphasized here. These modalities can make use of existing psychotherapeutic orientations such as psychodynamic and cognitive–behavioral therapy, which adapt to the interpersonal dimension necessary to interview and treat many individuals at a time. Extensive additional training may not be required for experienced psychotherapists who want to lend an interpersonal orientation to their practice.

Conjoint and group therapies are often brief, structured, and problem focused—characteristics which particularly well suit the current and the predicted trends in psychotherapy practice. These therapeutic modalities can easily be added to other clinical approaches, in the form of specific interventions tailored to specific problems. Using a diversity of approaches helps keep the clinician away from Mark Twain's adage, "If all you have is a hammer, everything looks like a nail."

The common nonspecific factors that make various individual psychotherapies effective are also at work in conjoint and group therapies. In particular, the relationship between the therapist and the people directly involved in the treatment is crucial. These interpersonal psychotherapies primarily aim to change relationships among family or group members in a therapeutic context of empathy and acceptance, which are curative factors common to various psychotherapeutic approaches.

The emphasis on relationships contradicts some models of conjoint and group therapy, as well as the commonly-held belief among clinicians that conjoint therapy, and some forms of group therapy, are just a set of behavioral manipulations and techniques. This belief is perpetuated by a tendency in some family and group therapists to ease into any new method available on the psychotherapy market.

Today's post-Freudian, postmodern period shows that relying exclusively on the individual and on individual therapy may be a weak strategy. The rekindled interest in Oriental philosophy may be seen as a manifestation of the need for larger philosophical and therapeutic schemes. Individual psychotherapy, as part of the structure built to fill the void from the decline of traditional support systems, has more or less failed in its function, especially toward the poor, the chronically mentally ill, children, and the elderly. Solutions are not likely to come from more money, more specialists, and more scientific approaches. These attempts will fail if they are not based on promoting a secure and supportive relationship between the sufferers and their relational environment.

Keeping in mind that no fascinating therapeutic approach will ever provide a complete answer to human problems, the interpersonal approach is quiet and difficult work that will not lead to miracle cures. It is common sense, down-to-earth work with realistic goals, unlikely to attract the flashy therapist seeking glamour. This type of intervention, however, allows people to confront problems face-to-face with no detour or artificiality. Life is witnessed as it is. The experience is usually rewarding for the people involved as well as for the therapist. It is a journey full of joy and pain, of wonder and uncertainty, as the experiential reality and some shadowy areas of the human condition are uncovered. The clinician can then make a significant contribution following the ecologist's dictum, "Think globally and act locally."

REFERENCES

Ackerman, N. W. (1958). *The psychodynamics of family life.* New York: Basic Books.

Adler, D. A. (1990). Personality disorders: Theory and psychotherapy. *New Directions for Mental Health Services, 47,* 17–42.

Alexander, J. F., Holtzworth-Munroe, A., & Jameson, P. (1994). The process and outcome of marital and family therapy: Research review and evaluation. In A. E. Bergin & S. L. Garfield (Eds.), *Handbook of psychotherapy and behavior change* (4th ed., pp. 595–630). New York: Wiley.

Alford, B. A., & Beck, A. T. (1997). *Integrative power of cognitive therapy.* New York: Guilford Press.

American Psychiatric Association (1989). *Treatment of psychiatric disorders. A task force report of the American Psychiatric Association.* Washington, DC: Author.

American Psychiatric Association (1994). *Diagnostic and statistical manual of mental disorders* (4th ed.). Washington, DC: Author.

Anchin, J. C., & Kiesler, D. J. (Eds.). (1982). *Handbook of interpersonal psychotherapy.* New York: Pergamon Press.

Anderson, C. M., Hogarty, G. E., & Reiss, D. J. (1980). Family treatment of adult schizophrenic patients: A psychoeducational approach. *Schizophrenia Bulletin, 6,* 490–505.

Anderson, W. T., & Hargrave, T. D. (1990). Contextual family therapy and older people: Building trust in the intergenerational family. *Journal of Family Therapy, 12,* 311–320.

Anthony, C. R., Zarit, S. H., & Gatz, M. (1988). Symptoms of psychological distress among caregivers of dementia patients. *Psychology and Aging, 3,* 25–48.

Asen, E. K. (1997). Family therapy with ageing families. In R. Jacoby & C. Oppenheimer (Eds.), *Psychiatry in the elderly* (2nd ed., pp. 269–281). Oxford: Oxford University Press.

Backlar, P. (1994). *The family face of schizophrenia: Practical counsel from America's leading experts.* New York: Jeremy P. Tarcher/Putnam.

Bagarozzi, D. A. (1996). *The couple and family in managed care.* New York: Brunner/Mazel.

Baumeister, R. (1987). How the self became a problem: A psychological review of historical research. *Journal of Personality and Social Psychology, 52,* 163–176.

Beardlee, W. R., Salt, P., Versage, E. V., Gladstone, T. R. G., Wright, E. J., & Rothbey, P. C. (1997). Sustained change in parents receiving preventive interventions for families with depression. *American Journal of Psychiatry, 154,* 510–515.

Bergin, A. E., & Garfield, S. L. (Eds.). (1994). *Handbook of psychotherapy and behavior change* (4th ed.). New York: Wiley.

Beutler, L. E., & Clarkin, J. F. (1990). *Systematic treatment selection.* New York: Brunner/Mazel.

Beutler, L. E., Machado, P. P., & Neufeldt, S. A. (1994). Therapist variables. In A. E. Bergin & S. L. Garfiel (Eds.), *Handbook of psychotherapy and behavior change* (4th ed., pp. 229–269). New York: Wiley.

Blos, P. (1985). *Son and father: Before and beyond the Oedipus complex.* New York: Free Press.

Boszormenyi-Nagy, I., Grunebaum, J., & Ulrich, D (1991). Contextual therapy. In A. S. Gurman & D. P. Kniskern (Eds.), *Handbook of family therapy* (Vol. II, pp. 200–238). New York: Brunner/Mazel.

Boyum, L. A., & Parke, R. D. (1999). Family. In W. K. Silverman & T. H. Ollendick (Eds.), *Developmental issues in the clinical treatment of children* (pp. 141–155). Boston: Allyn and Bacon.

Bray, J. H., & Jouriles, E. N. (1995). Treatment of marital conflict and prevention of divorce. *Journal of Marital and Family therapy, 21,* 461–473.

Bronfenbrenner, U. (1986). Ecology of the family as a context for human development: Research perspectives. *Developmental Psychology, 22,* 723–742.

Budman, S. H., & Gurman, A. S. (1988). *Theory and Practice of Brief Therapy.* New York: Guilford.

Budman, S. H., Cooley, S., Demby, A., & Koppenaal, G. (1996). A model of time-effective group psychotherapy for patients with personality disorders: The clinical model. *International Journal of Group Psychotherapy, 46,* 329–355.

Budman, S. H., Demby. A., Soldz, S., & Merry, J. (1996). Time-limited group psychotherapy for patients with personality disorders: Outcomes and dropouts. *International Journal of Group Psychotherapy, 46,* 357–377.

Bugental, J. F. T., & Sterling, M. M. (1995). Existential-humanistic psychotherapy: New perspectives. In A. S. Gurman & S. B. Messer

(Eds.), *Essential psychotherapies: Theory and practice* (pp. 226–260). New York: Guilford Press.

Buglass, D., Clarke, J., Henderson, A. S. et al. (1977). A study of agoraphobic housewifes. *Psychological Medicine, 7,* 73–86.

Butler, R. N., & Lewis, M. I. (1991). *Aging and mental health.* New York: Merrill.

Campbell, T. L., & Patterson, J. (1995). The effectiveness of family interventions in the treatment of physical illness. *Journal of Marital and Family Therapy, 21,* 545–583.

Casimir, G. J., & Morrison, B. J. (1993). Rethinking work with "multicultural population." *Community Mental Health Journal, 29,* 547–559.

Chamberlain, P., & Rosicky, J. G. (1995). The effectiveness of family therapy in the treatment of adolescents with conduct disorders and delinquency. *Journal of Marital and Family Therapy, 21,* 441–459.

Clarkin, J. F., Marziali, E., & Munroe-Blum, H. (1991). Group and family treatments for borderline personality disorder. *Hospital and Community Psychiatry, 42,* 1038–1043.

Clarkin, J. F., Glick, I. D., Haas, G. L., Spencer, J.H., Lewis, A. B., Peyser, J., DeMane, N., Good-Ellis, M., Harris, E., & Lestelle, V. (1990). A randomized clinical trial of inpatient family intervention. V: Results for affective disorders. *Journal of Affective Disorders, 18,* 17–28.

Combrinck-Graham, L. (1996). Family psychotherapy. In L. J. Dickstein, M. B. Riba, & J. M. Oldham (Eds.), *Review of psychiatry,* (Vol. 15, pp. 129–150). Washington, DC: American Psychiatric Press.

Corder, B., Whiteside, R., & Haizlip, T. (1981). A study of curative factors in group psychotherapy with adolescents. *International Journal of Group Psychotherapy, 31,* 345–354.

Cornes, C. & Frank, E. (1996). Interpersonal psychotherapy. In L. J. Dickstein, M. B. Riba, & J. M. Oldham (Eds.), *Review of psychiatry* (Vol. 15, pp. 91–107). Washington, DC: American Psychiatric Press.

Corrigan, P. W., Liberman, R. P., & Engel, J. D. (1990). From noncompliance to collaboration in the treatment of schizophrenia. *Hospital and Community Psychiatry, 41,* 1203–1211.

Cushman, P. (1992). Psychotherapy to 1992: A historically situated interpretation. In D. K. Friedheim (Ed.), *History of psychotherapy: A century of change* (pp. 21–64). Washington, DC: American Psychological Association.

Cushman, P. (1995). *Constructing the self, constructing America: A cultural history of psychotherapy.* Reading, MA: Addison-Wesley.

Deimling, G. T., & Bass, D. M. (1986). Symptoms of mental impairment among elderly adults and their effects on family caregivers. *Journal of Gerontology, 41,* 778–784.

Diamond, G. S., Serrano, A. C., Dickey, M., & Sonis, W. A. (1996). Current status of family-based outcome and process research. *Journal of the American Academy of Child and Adolescent Psychiatry, 35,* 6–16.

Dies, R. R. (1993). Research on group psychotherapy: Overview and clinical applications. In A. Alonso & H. I. Swiller (Eds.), *Group therapy in clinical practice* (pp. 473–518). Washington, DC: American Psychiatric Press.

Dies, R. R. (1994). Therapist variables in group psychotherapy research. In A. Fuhriman & G. M. Burlingame (Eds.), *Handbook of group psychotherapy* (pp. 114–154). New York: Wiley.

Doidge, N. (1997). Empirical evidence for the efficacy of psychotherapies and psychoanalysis: An overview. *Psychoanalytic Inquiry,* suppl., 102–150.

Dow, J. (1986). Universal aspects of symbolic healing: A theoretical synthesis. *American Anthropologist, 88,* 56–69.

Downey, G., & Coyne, J. C. (1990). Children of depressed parents: An integrative review. *Psychological Bulletin, 108,* 50–76.

Edwards, M. A., & Steinglass, P. (1995). Family therapy treatment outcomes for alcoholism. *Journal of Marital and Family Therapy, 21,* 475–509.

Ehrenwald, J. (Ed.). (1976). *The history of psychotherapy: From healing magic to encounter.* New York: Jason Aronson.

Eisenck, H. J. (1952). The effects of psychotherapy: An evaluation. *Journal of Consulting Psychology, 16,* 319–324.

Emslie, G. J., Rush, J., Weinberg, W. A., & Kowatch, R. A., Hughes, C. W., Carmody, T., & Rintelmann, J. (1997). A double-blind, randomized, placebo-controlled trial of fluoxetine in children and adolescents with depression. *Archives of General Psychiatry, 54,* 1031–1037.

Estrada, A. U., & Pinsof, W. M. (1995). The effectiveness of family therapies for selected behavioral disorders of childhood. *Journal of Marital and Family Therapy, 21,* 403–440.

Falloon, I. R. H., Boyd, J. L., McGill, C. W., Razani, J., Moss, H. B., & Gilderman, A. M. (1982). Family management in the prevention of exacerbations of schizophrenia. *New England Journal of Medicine, 306,* 1437–1440.

Feldman, L. B. (1992). *Integrating individual and family therapy.* New York: Brunner/Mazel.

Feldman, R. B., & Guttman, H. A. (1984). Families of borderline patients: Literal-minded parents, borderline parents, and parental protectiveness. *American Journal of Psychiatry, 141,* 1392–1396.

Fogel, B. S., & Sadavoy, J. (1996). Somatoform and personality disorders. In J. Sadavoy, L. W. Lazarus, L. F. Jarvik, & G. T. Grossberg

(Eds.), *Comprehensive review of geriatric psychiatry-11* (2nd ed., pp. 637–658). Washington, DC: American Psychiatric Press.

Ford, D. H., & Urban, H. B. (Eds.). (1998). *Contemporary models of psychotherapy: A comparative analysis* (2nd ed.). New York: Wiley.

Foucault, M. (1973). *Histoire de la Folie à l'Âge Classique* [Madness and civilization: A history of insanity in the age of reason]. Paris: Gallimard.

Frank, J. D. (1982). Psychotherapy in America today. In R. Goldfried (Ed.), *Converging themes in psychotherapy* (pp. 78–93). New York: Springer.

Freud, S. (1919). Lines of advance in psycho-analytic therapy. *Standard Edition, 17,* 159–168.

Fuhriman, A., & Burlingame, G. M. (Eds.). (1994). *Handbook of group psychotherapy.* New York: Wiley.

Fuhriman, A., Drescher, S., Hanson, E. et al. (1986). Refining the measurement of curativeness: An empirical approach. *Small Group Behavior, 17,* 186–201.

Gabbard, G. O. (1994). *Psychodynamic psychiatry in clinical practice: The DSM-IV edition.* Washington, DC: American Psychiatric Association.

Garfield, S. L. (1986). Research on client variables in psychotherapy. In A. E. Bergin & S. L. Garfield (Eds.), *Handbook of psychotherapy and behavior change* (3rd ed., pp. 213–256). New York: Wiley.

Garfield, S. L. (1994). Research on client variables in psychotherapy. In A. E. Bergin & S. L. Garfield (Eds.), *Handbook of psychotherapy and behavior change* (4th ed., pp. 190–228). New York: Wiley.

Garfield, S. L., & Bergin, A. E. (1994). Introduction and historical overview. In A. E. Bergin & S. L. Garfield (Eds.), *Handbook of psychotherapy and behavior change* (4th ed., pp. 3–18). New York: Wiley.

Gartner, A., & Reissman, F. (1977). *From self-help in the human services.* San Francisco: Jossey-Bass.

Gergen, K. J. (1992). Toward a postmodern psychology. In S. Kvale (Ed.), *Psychology and postmodernism* (pp. 1–16). Newbury Park, CA: Sage.

Glantz, K., & Pearce, J. (1989). *Exiles from Eden. Psychotherapy from an evolutionary perspective.* New York: Norton.

Goldner, V. (1991). Feminism and systemic practice: Two critical traditions in transition. *Journal of Family Therapy, 13,* 95–104.

Golstein, M. Z. (1996). Families of older adults. In J. Sadavoy, L. W. Lazarus, L. F. Jarvik, & G. T. Grossberg (Eds.), *Comprehensive review of geriatric psychiatry-11* (2nd ed., pp. 881–906). Washington, DC: American Psychiatric Press.

Goldstein, M. J., & Miklowitz, D. J. (1995). The effectiveness of psycho-educational family therapy in the treatment of schizophrenic disorders. *Journal of Marital and Family Therapy, 21,* 361–376.

Goodman, G., & Jacobs, M. K. (1994). The self-help, mutual-support group. In A. Fuhriman & G. M. Burlingame (Eds.), *Handbook of group psychotherapy* (pp. 489–526). New York: Wiley.

Greenberg, L., Elliott, R., & Lietaer, G. (1994). Research on experiential psychotherapies. In A. E. Bergin & S. L. Garfield (Eds.), *Handbook of psychotherapy and behavior change* (4th ed., pp. 509–539). New York: Wiley.

Group for the Advancement of Psychiatry (GAP) Committee on Therapy. (1992). *Psychotherapy in the future. Group for the advancement of psychiatry* (Rep. No. 133). Washington, DC: American Psychiatric Press.

Gunderson, J. G. (1984). *Borderline personality disorders.* Washington, DC: American Psychiatric Press.

Gunderson, J. G., Berkowitz, C., & Ruiz-Sancho, A. (1997). Families of borderline patients: A psychoeducational approach. *Bulletin of the Menninger Clinic, 61,* 446–457.

Gunderson, J. G., Frank, A. F., Ronningstam, E. F., Wachter, S., Lynch, V. J., & Wolf, P. J. (1989). Early discontinuance of borderline patients from psychotherapy. *Journal of Nervous and Mental Disease, 177,* 38–42.

Gurfein, H. N., & Stutman, G. F. (1993). Group psychotherapy with the elderly. In H. I. Kaplan & B. J. Sadock (Eds.), *Comprehensive group psychotherapy* (3rd ed., pp. 584–597). Baltimore, MD: Williams and Wilkins.

Haley, J. (1976). *Problem solving therapy: New strategies for effective family therapy.* San Francisco: Jossey-Bass.

Hanson, J. G., & Rapp, C. A. (1992). Families' perceptions of community mental health programs for their relatives with a severe mental illness. *Community Mental Health Journal, 28,* 181–197.

Hargrave, T. D., & Anderson, W. T. (1992). *Finishing well. Aging and reparation in the intergenerational family.* New York: Brunner/Mazel.

Hatcher, S. L., & Hatcher, R. L. (1983). Set a place for Elijah: Problems of the spouses and parents of psychotherapy patients. *Psychotherapy: Theory, Research and Practice, 20,* 75–80.

Hatfield, A . B., & Lefley, H. P. (1993). *Surviving mental illness: Stress, coping and adaptation.* New York: Guilford Press.

Henry, W. P., Strupp, H. S., Schacht, T, A., & Gaston, L. (1994). Psychodynamic approaches. In A. E. Bergin & S. L. Garfield (Eds.), *Handbook of psychotherapy and behavior change* (4th ed., pp. 467–508). New York: Wiley.

Hogue, A., & Liddle, H. A. (1999). Family-based preventive intervention: An approach to preventing substance use and antisocial behavior. *American Journal of Orthopsychiatry, 69,* 278–293.

Holmes, J. (1994). Psychotherapy—A luxury the NHS cannot afford? *British Medical Journal, 309*, 1070–1071.

Holmes, J., & Lindley, R. (1989). *The values of psychotherapy.* Oxford: Oxford University Press.

Hooley, J. M., & Teasdale, J, D. (1989). Predictors of relapse in unipolar depressives: Expressed emotion, marital distress, and perceived criticism. *Journal of Abnormal Psychology, 98*, 229–235.

Horwitz, L., Gabbard, G. O., Allen, J. G., Frieswyk, S. H., Colson, D. B., Newsom, G. E., & Coyne, L. (1996). *Borderline personality disorder: Tailoring the psychotherapy to the patient.* Washington, DC: American Psychiatric Press.

Howard, K. I., Kopta, S. M., Krause, M. S., & Orlinsky, D. E. (1986). The dose-effect relationship in psychotherapy. *American Psychologist, 41*, 159–164.

Hunsley, J., & Lee, C. M. (1995). The marital effects of individually oriented psychotherapy: Is there evidence for the deterioration hypothesis? *Clinical Psychology Review, 15*, 1–22.

Jacobson, N. S., & Addis, M. E. (1993). Research on couples and couple therapy: What do we know? Where are we going? *Journal of Consulting and Clinical Psychology, 61*, 85–93.

Jacobson, N. S., Dobson, K., Fruzzetti, A. E., Schmaling, K. B., & Salusky, S. (1991). Marital therapy as a treatment for depression. *Journal of Consulting and Clinical Psychology, 59*, 547–557.

Katz, A. H. (1993). *Self-help in America: A social movement perspective.* New York: Twayne.

Kazdin, A. E. (1994a). Methodology, design, and evaluation in psychotherapy research. In A. E. Bergin & S. L. Garfield (Eds.), *Handbook of psychotherapy and behavior change* (4th ed., pp. 19–71). New York: Wiley.

Kazdin, A. E. (1994b). Psychotherapy for children and adolescents. In A. E. Bergin & S. L. Garfield (Eds.), *Handbook of psychotherapy and behavior change* (4th ed., pp. 543–594). New York: Wiley.

Keitner, G. I., & Miller, I. W. (1990). Family functioning and major depression: An overview. *American Journal of Psychiatry, 147*, 1128–1137.

Kiesler, D. J. (1982). Interpersonal theory for personality and psychotherapy. In J. C. Anchin & D. J. Kiesler (Eds.), *Handbook of interpersonal psychotherapy.* New York: Pergamon Press.

Klerman, G. L., & Weissman, M. M. (Eds.). (1993). *New applications of interpersonal psychotherapy.* Washington, DC: American Psychiatric Press.

Klerman, G. L., Weissman, M. M., Rounsaville, B. J., & Chevron, E. S. (1984). *Interpersonal psychotherapy of depression.* New York: Basic Books.

Kniskern, D. P., & Gurman, A. S. (1985), A marital and family therapy perspective on deterioration in psychotherapy. In D. T. Mays & C. M. Franks (Eds.), *Negative outcome in psychotherapy* (pp. 106–118). New York: Springer.

Kojima, H. (1984). A significant stride toward the comparative study of control. *American Psychologist, 39,* 972–973.

Kymissis, P. (1993). Group therapy with adolescents. In H. I. Kaplan & B. J. Sadock (Eds.), *Comprehensive group therapy* (3rd ed., pp. 577–584). Baltimore: Williams and Wilkins.

La Greca, A. M., & Prinstein, M. J. (1999). Peer group. In W. K. Silverman & T. H. Ollendick (Eds.), *Developmental issues in the clinical treatment of children* (pp. 171–198). Boston: Allyn and Bacon.

Lambert, M. J., & Bergin, A. E. (1994). The effectiveness of psychotherapy. In A. E. Bergin & S. L. Garfield (Eds.), *Handbook of psychotherapy and behavior change* (4th ed., pp. 143–189). New York: Wiley.

Lambert, M. J., & Hill, C. E. (1994). Assessing psychotherapy outcomes and process. In A. E. Bergin & S. L. Garfield (Eds.), *Handbook of psychotherapy and behavior change* (4th ed., pp. 72–113). New York: Wiley.

Lansky, M. R. (1985). Marital therapy for narcissistic disorders. In N. S. Jacobson & A. S. Gurman (Eds.), *Clinical handbook of marital therapy* (pp. 557–574). New York: Guilford Press.

Lazarus, L. W., & Sadavoy, J. (1996). Individual psychotherapy. In J. Sadavoy, L. W. Lazarus, L. F. Jarvik, & G. T. Grossberg (Eds.), *Comprehensive review of geriatric psychiatry-11* (2nd ed., pp. 819–850). Washington, DC: American Psychiatric Press.

Lee, D. T. (1995). Professional underutilization of Recovery, Inc. *Psychiatric Rehabilitation Journal, 19,* 63–70.

Lefebvre, M., & Hunsley, J. (1994). Couples's accounts of the effects of individual psychotherapy. *Psychotherapy, 31,* 183–189.

Lefley, H. P. (1996). *Family caregiving in mental illness.* Thousand Oaks, CA: Sage.

Lefley, H. P., & Bestman, E. W. (1984). Community mental health and minorities. A multi-ethnic approach. In S. Sue & T. Moore (Eds.), *The pluralistic society. A community mental health perspective* (pp. 116–148). New York: Human Sciences Press.

Lerner, R. M., Villarruel, F. A., & Castellino, D. R. (1999). Adolescence. In W. K. Silverman & T. H. Ollendick (Eds.), *Developmental issues in the clinical treatment of children* (pp. 125–136). Boston: Allyn and Bacon.

Leszcz, M. (1996). Group therapy. In J. Sadavoy, L. W. Lazarus, L. F. Jarvik, & G. T. Grossberg (Eds.), *Comprehensive review of geriatric psychiatry-11* (2nd ed., pp. 851–879). Washington, DC: American Psychiatric Press.

Leszcz, M. (1998). Guidelines for the practice of group psychotherapy. In P. Cameron, J. Ennis & J. Deadman (Eds.), *Standards and guidelines for the psychotherapies* (pp. 199–227). Toronto: University of Toronto Press.

Lewis, J. M. (1998). For better or worse: Interpersonal relationships and individual outcome. *American Journal of Psychiatry, 155,* 582–589.

Liddle, H. A., & Dakof, G. A. (1995). Efficacy of family therapy for drug abuse: Promising but not definitive. *Journal of Marital and Family Therapy, 21,* 511–543.

Lieberman, M. A. (1994). Growth groups in the 1980s: Mental health implications. In A. Fuhriman & G. M. Burlingame (Eds.), *Handbook of group psychotherapy* (pp. 527–558). New York: Wiley.

Lieberman, M. A., & Snowden, L. R. (1994). Problems in assessing prevalence and membership characteristics of self-help group participants. In T. J. Powell (Ed.), *Understanding the self-help organization. Frameworks and findings* (pp. 32–49). Thousand Oaks, CA: Sage Publications.

Linehan, M. M., Armstrong, H, E., Suarez, A., Allmon, D., & Heard, H. L. (1991). Cognitive-behavioral treatment of chronically parasuicidal borderline patients. *Archives of General Psychiatry, 48,* 1060–1064.

Liotti, G. (1988). Attachment and cognition: A guideline for the reconstruction of early pathogenic experiences in cognitive psychotherapy. In C. Perris, I. M. Blackburn, & H. Perris (Eds.), *Cognitive psychotherapy: Theory and practice* (pp. 62–79). New York: Springer-Verlag.

Longino, C. F., Jr., & Mittelmark, M. B. (1996). Sociodemographic aspects. In J. Sadavoy, L. W. Lazarus, L. F. Jarvik, & G. T. Grossberg (Eds.), *Comprehensive review of geriatric psychiatry-11* (2nd ed., pp. 135–152). Washington, DC: American Psychiatric Press.

Luborsky, L., Docherty, J. P., & Miller, N. E., et al. (1993). What's here and what's ahead in dynamic therapy research and practice? In N. E. Miller, L. Luborsky, J. P. Barber, & J. P. Docherty (Eds.), *Psychodynamic treatment research: A handbook for clinical practice* (pp. 536–553). New York: Basic Books.

MacKenzie, K. R. (1990). *Introduction to time-limited group psychotherapy.* Washington, DC: American Psychiatric Press.

MacKenzie, K. R. (1995). Rationale for group psychotherapy in managed care. In K. R. MacKenzie (Ed.), *Effective use of group therapy in managed care* (pp. 1–25). Washington, DC: American Psychiatric Press.

MacKenzie, K. R. (1996). The time-limited psychotherapies: An overview. In L. J. Dickstein, M. B. Riba, & J. M. Oldham (Eds.), *Review of psychiatry* (Vol. 15, pp. 11–21). Washington, DC: American Psychiatric Press.

Malan, D. H., Balfour, F. H. G., Hood, V. G., & Shooter, A. M. N. (1976). Group psychotherapy. A long-term follow-up study. *Archives of General Psychiatry, 33,* 1303–1315.

Markus, E., Lange, A., & Pettigrew, T. F. (1990). Effectiveness of family therapy: A meta-analysis. *Journal of Family Therapy, 12,* 205–221.

Marziali, E. A., & Munroe-Blum, H. (1994). *Interpersonal group psychotherapy for borderline personality disorder.* New York: Basic Books.

McFarlane, W. R., Lukens, E., Link, B., Dushay, R., Deakins, S. A., Newmark, M., Dunne, E. J., Horen, B., & Toran, J. (1995). Multiple-family groups and psychoeducation in the treatment of schizophrenia. *Archives of General Psychiatry, 52,* 679–687.

Meissen, G. J., & Warren, M. L. (1994). The self-help clearinghouse: A new development in action research for community psychology. In T. J. Powell (Ed.), *Understanding the self-help organization. Frameworks and findings* (pp. 190–211). Thousand Oaks, CA: Sage Publications.

Minuchin, S. (1974). *Families and family therapy.* Cambridge, MA: Harvard University Press.

Minuchin, S., Montalvo, B., Guerney, B. G., Rosman, B. L., & Schumer, F. (1967). *Families of the slums: An exploration of their structure and treatment.* New York: Basic Books.

Murata, P. J., & Kane, R. L. (1987). Do families get family care? *Journal of the American Medical Association, 257,* 1912–1915.

Narrow, W. E., Regier, D. A., Rae, D. S., Manderscheid, R. W., & Locke, B. Z. (1993). Use of services by persons with mental and addictive disorders. *Archives of General Psychiatry, 50,* 95–107.

Nichols, M. P. (1988). *The power of the family.* New York: Fireside/ Simon and Schuster.

Nichols, M. P., & Minuchin, S. (1999). Short-term structural family therapy with couples. In J. M. Donovan et al. (Eds.), *Short-term couple therapy* (pp. 124–143). New York: Guilford Press.

Nichols, M. P., & Schwartz, R. C. (1998). *Family therapy. Concepts and methods* (4th ed.). Boston: Allyn and Bacon.

Norcross, J. C., & Newman, C. F. (1992). Psychotherapy integration: Setting the context. In J. C. Norcross & M. R. Goldfried (Eds.), *Handbook of psychotherapy integration* (pp. 3–45). New York: Basic Books.

Norcross, J. C., Alford, B. A., & DeMichele, J. T. (1992). The future of psychotherapy: Delphi data and concluding observations. *Psychotherapy, 29,* 150–158.

North, C. S., Pollio, D. E., Sachar, B., Hong, B., Isenberg, K., & Bufe, G. (1998). The family as a caregiver: A group psychoeducation model for schizophrenia. *American Journal of Orthopsychiatry, 68,* 39–46.

Olfson, M., & Pincus, H. A. (1994). Outpatient psychotherapy in the United States, 11: Patterns of utilization. *American Journal of Psychiatry, 151,* 1289–1294.

Paris, J. (1996). *Social factors in the personality disorders. A biopsychosocial approach to etiology and treatment.* New York: Cambridge University Press.

Patterson, G, R., Capaldi, D., & Bank, L. (1991). An early starter model predicting delinquency. In D. J. Peppler & K. H. Rubin (Eds.), *The development and treatment of childhood aggression* (pp. 139–168). Hillsdale, NJ: Lawrence Erlbaum.

Perkins, R. E., & Poynton, C. F. (1990). Group counselling for relatives of hospitalized presenile dementia patients: A controlled study. *British Journal of Clinical Psychology, 29,* 287–295.

Pinsof, W. M., & Wynne, L .C. (1995). The efficacy of marital and family therapy: An empirical review, conclusions, and recommendations. *Journal of Marital and Family Therapy, 21,* 585–613.

Piper, W. E. (1993). Group therapy research. In H. I. Kaplan & B. J. Sadock (Eds.), *Comprehensive group psychotherapy* (3rd ed., pp. 673–681). Baltimore: Williams and Wilkins.

Powell, T. J. (1994). Self-help research and policy issues. In T. J. Powell (Ed.), *Understanding self-help organization* (pp. 1–19). Thousand Oaks, CA: Sage Publications.

Prince, S. E., & Jacobson, N. S. (1995). A review and evaluation of marital and family therapies for affective disorders. *Journal of Marital and Family Therapy, 21,* 377–401.

Procter, H., & Pieczora, R. (1993). A family oriented community mental health centre. In J. Carpenter & A. Treacher (Eds.), *Using family therapy in the 90s* (pp. 131–144). Oxford, UK: Blackwell.

Ratna, L., & Davis, J. (1984). Family therapy with the elderly mentally ill: Some strategies and techniques. *British Journal of Psychiatry, 145,* 311–315.

Reiss, D., Hetherington, E. M., Plomin, R., Howe, G. W., Simmens, S. J., Henderson, S. H., O'Connor, T. J., Bussell, D. A., Anderson, E. R., & Law, T. (1995). Genetic questions for environmental studies. Differential parenting and psychopathology in adolescence. *Archives of General Psychiatry, 52,* 925–936.

Reissman, F., & Carroll, D. (1995). *Redifining self-help: Policy and practice.* San Francisco: Jossey-Bass.

Robinson, L. A., Berman, J. S., & Neimeyer, R. A. (1990). Psychotherapy for the treatment of depression: A comprehensive review of controlled outcome research. *Psychological Bulletin, 108,* 30.

Rogers, C. R. (1951). *Client-centered therapy. Its current practice, implications, and theory.* Boston: Houghton Mifflin.

Rosenbaum, M., Lakin, M., & Roback, H. B. (1992). Psychotherapy in groups. In D. K. Freedheim, H. J. Freudenberg, J. W. Kessler, S. B. Messer, D. R. Peterson, H. E. Strupp, & P. L. Wachtel (Eds.), *History of psychotherapy. A century of change* (pp. 695–724). Washington, DC: American Psychological Association.

Roth, B. E., Stone, W. N., & Kibel, H. D. (1990). The difficult patient in group psychotherapy. In B. E. Roth, W. N. Stone, & H. D. Kibel (Eds.), *American Group Psychotherapy Association, Monograph 6.* Madison, CT: International Universities Press.

Russell, G. F. M., Szmukler, G., Dare, C., & Eisler, I. (1987). An evaluation of family therapy in anorexia nervosa and bulimia nervosa. *Archives of General Psychiatry, 44,* 1047–1056.

Rutter, M., & Quinton, D. (1984). Parental psychiatric disorder: Effects on children. *Psychological Medicine, 14,* 853–880.

Sadavoy, J. (1994). Integrated psychotherapy for the elderly. *Canadian Journal of Psychiatry, 39* (Supp. 1), 19–26.

Sampson, E. E. (1993). *Celebrating the other: A dialogic account of human nature.* Boulder, CO: Westview Press.

Schacht, T. E. (1984). The varieties of integrative experience. In H. Arkowitz, S. B. Messer et al. (Eds.), *Psychoanalytic therapy and behavior therapy. Is integration possible?* (pp. 107–131). New York: Plenum Press.

Schulz, P. M., Schulz, S. C., Hamer, R., Resnick, R. J., Friedel, R. O., & Goldberg, S. C. (1985). The impact of borderline and schizotypal personality disorders on patients and their families. *Hospital and Community Psychiatry, 36,* 879–881.

Scogin, F., & McElreath, L. (1994). Efficacy of psychosocial treatments for geriatric depression: A quantitative review. *Journal of Consulting and Clinical Psychology, 62,* 69–74.

Segal, B. M., & Weideman, R. (1995). Outpatient groups for patients with personality disorders. In K. R. MacKenzie (Ed.), *Effective use of group therapy in managed care* (pp. 147–164). Washington, DC: American Psychiatric Press.

Shadish, W. R., Ragsdale, K., Glaser, R. R., & Montgomery, L. M. (1995). The efficacy and effectiveness of marital and family therapy: A perspective from meta-analysis. *Journal of Marital and Family Therapy, 21,* 345–360.

Shapiro, T., & Emde, R. (Eds.). (1995). *Research in psychoanalysis. Process, development, outcome.* Madison, CT: International Universities Press.

Shea, M. T., Elkin, I., Imber, S. D., Sotsky, S. M., Watkins, J. T., Collins, J. F., Pilkonis, P. A., Beckham, E., Glass, D. R., Dolan, R. T., & Parloff, M. B. (1992). Course of depressive symptoms over follow-up: Findings from the National Institute of Mental Health Treatment of Depression Collaborative Research Program. *Archives of General Psychiatry, 49,* 782–787.

Shields, C. G., Wynne, L. C., McDaniel, S. H., & Gowinski, B. A. (1994). The marginalization of family therapy: A historical and continuing problem. *Journal of Marital and Family Therapy, 20,* 117–138.

Slavson, S. R. (1943). *An introduction to group therapy.* New York: International Universities Press.

Spitz, H. I. (1996). *Group psychotherapy and managed mental health care.* New York: Brunner/Mazel.

Stanton, M. D., & Shadish, W. R. (1997). Outcome, attrition, and family-couples treatment for drug abuse: A meta-analysis and review of the controlled, comparative studies. *Psychological Bulletin, 122,* 170–191.

Stein, A., Kibel, H. D., Fidler, J., & Spitz, H. (1982). The group therapies. In J. M. Lewis & G. Usdin (Eds.), *Treatment planning in psychiatry* (pp. 45–85). Washington, DC: American Psychiatric Press.

Steinberg, L. (1990). Interdependency in the family: Autonomy, conflict, and harmony. In R. Feldman & G. Elliot (Eds.), *At the threshold: The developing adolescent* (pp. 255–276). Cambridge, MA: Harvard University Press.

Stolorow, R. D., & Atwood, G. E. (1992). *Contexts of being: The intersubjective foundations of psychological life.* Hillsdale, NJ: Analytic Press.

Stone, W. N. (1996). *Group psychotherapy for people with chronic mental illness.* New York: Guilford Press.

Sue, S., & Zane, N. (1987). The role of culture and cultural techniques in psychotherapy. *American Psychologist, 42,* 37–45.

Sue, S., Zane, N., & Young, K. (1994). Research on psychotherapy with culturally diverse populations. In A. E. Bergin & S. L. Garfield (Eds.), *Handbook of psychotherapy and behavior change* (4th ed., pp. 783–817). New York: Wiley.

Sullivan, H. S. (1953). *The interpersonal theory of psychiatry.* New York: Norton.

Sutherland, J. D. (1981). Psychoanalysis as a form of psychotherapy. In M. Dongier & E. D. Wittkower (Eds.), *Divergent views in psychiatry* (pp. 100–131). Hagerstown, MD: Harper and Row.

Szapocznik, J., Perez-Vidal, A., Brickman, A. L., Foote, F. H., Santisteban, D., & Hervis, O. (1988). Engaging adolescent drug abusers and their families in treatment. *Journal of Consulting and Clinical Psychology, 36,* 552–557.

Taylor, C. (1989). *Sources of the self: The making of the modern identity.* Cambridge, MA: Harvard University Press.

Taylor, C. (1992). *Malaise of modernity.* Cambridge, MA: Harvard University Press.

Tillitski, C. J. (1990). A meta-analysis of estimated effect sizes for group versus individual control treatment. *International Journal of Group Psychotherapy, 40,* 215.

Vandenhos, G. R., Cummings, N. A., & Deleon, P. H. (1992). A century of psychotherapy: Economic and environmental influences. In D. K. Freidheim (Ed.), *History of psychotherapy. A century of change* (pp. 65–102). Washington, DC: American Psychological Association.

Villeneuve, C., Bérubé, H., Ouellet, R., & Delorme, A. (1996). Prevention concerning mental health: The adolescent's perspective. *Canadian Journal of Psychiatry, 41,* 392–399.

Villeneuve, C., & Guttman, H. A. (1994). Psychodynamic family therapy with narcissistic borderline parents. *Journal of Family Psychotherapy, 5,* 41–56.

von Bertalanffy, L. (1968). *General system theory.* New York: Braziller.

Wachtel, E. F., & Wachtel, P. L. (1986). *Family dynamics in individual psychotherapy: A guide to clinical strategies.* New York: Guilford Press.

Wachtel, P. L. (1987). *Action and insight.* New York: Guilford Press.

Wachtel, P. L., & McKinney, M. K. (1992). Cyclical psychodynamics and integrative psychodynamic psychotherapy. In J. C. Norcross & M. R. Goldfried (Eds.), *Handbook of psychotherapy integration* (pp. 335–370). New York: Basic Books.

Watzlawick, P., Beavin, J. H., & Jackson, D. D. (1967). *Pragmatics of human communications.* New York: Norton.

Weber, J. J., Solomon, M., & Bachrach, H. M. (1985). Characteristics of psychoanalytic clinic patients: Report of the Columbia Psychoanalytic Center Research Project. *International Review of Psychoanalysis, 12,* 13–26.

Weiner, M. F. (1992). Group therapy reduces medical and psychiatric hospitalization. *International Journal of Group Psychotherapy, 42,* 267–275.

Weissman, M. M., & Paykel, E. S. (1994). *The depressed woman: A study of social relationships.* Chicago, IL: University of Chicago Press.

Wilkes, T. C. R., Belsher, G., Rush, A. J., & Frank, E. (1994). *Cognitive therapy for depressed adolescents.* New York: Guilford Press.

Wortman, C., & Silver, R. C. (1989). The myth of coping with loss. *Journal of Consulting and Clinical Psychology, 57,* 349–357.

Wynne, L. C., McDaniel, S. H., & Weber, T. T. (1987). Professional politics and the concepts of family therapy, family consultation, and system consultation. *Family Process, 26,* 153–166.

Yalom, I. D. (1980). *Existential psychotherapy.* New York: Basic Books.

Yalom, I. D. (1995). *The theory and practice of group psychotherapy* (4th ed.). New York: Basic Books.

INDEX